Why Ben?

Why Ben?

A sister's story of heartbreak and
love for the brother she lost

BROOKE KINSELLA

POCKET
BOOKS

LONDON • SYDNEY • NEW YORK • TORONTO

First published in Great Britain by Pocket Books, 2009
An imprint of Simon & Schuster UK Ltd
A CBS COMPANY

3 5 7 9 10 8 6 4

Simon & Schuster UK Ltd
1st Floor
222 Gray's Inn Road
London WC1X 8HB

www.simonandschuster.co.uk

Simon & Schuster Australia
Sydney

A CIP catalogue record for this book is available
from the British Library.

ISBN: 978-1-84739-847-5

Typeset by M Rules
Printed by CPI Cox & Wyman, Reading, Berkshire RG1 8EX

To my beautiful, beautiful family –
Mum, Dad, Jade, Georgia and Ben
Your strength and courage throughout this awful nightmare
has amazed me.
Even though we have been torn apart,
Let's hold on for the day when we are put back together.
I love you all more than you will ever know.

Contents

Chapter 1

I walk in and find you asleep.

This isn't unusual – you're always getting into trouble for being asleep when you should be doing much more important things. There's a running joke we have that you could fall asleep any time, any place. It's hard to wake you to tell you off, though, as you make sleeping look like an art – spread diagonally across any space, arms and legs everywhere, usually with one pet or another draped across you and the most beautiful, peaceful smile on your face. I wouldn't want to wake you then.

But this is very different.

I walk in to find you asleep but you're not in your own bed. And instead of being sprawled out, reaching for as much space as your skinny body can cover, you are lying completely stiff and still. And instead of having one of your beloved pets to keep you company, there are wires and machines and bandages. And instead of looking beautiful and peaceful, you look like you're having a terrible nightmare. I really want to wake you up now.

Why Ben?

We all crowd round you and we cry and we sob, and we beg to be able to turn back time. We beg to change places. We beg them to try one more thing, press one more button, do anything to bring you back again. But there is nothing more they can do – they can't take that look off your face, they can't stop the cold and the yellow that is seeping into your body and they can't wake you up either.

They tell us to take as much time as we need.

We soak up every bit of you. We try to memorize you and even though we don't want to remember you like this, you are still ours – we can still touch you and kiss you and smell you – underneath the cold, underneath the yellow, underneath the smell of this awful, awful place we try to find you.

So that is what we do – we rotate around you, touching every part of you, kissing every bit of you, covering every inch of you with our tears. And every time we try to leave, we remember another place we didn't kiss and we have to come running back.

We don't want to leave you but you have already left us – not through choice, you were taken, stolen, snatched away, but we will deal with that later. Right now, all I want is to pick you up and run away from here – put you in your own bed, wrap you in your duvet, bring you home where you belong. I think about how cold you are, and where they will put your little body next and my heart breaks all over again.

I can't believe this has happened to us, has happened to you. I become obsessed with time – five minutes ago you were still here, ten minutes ago you were still alive. I look at our broken family and I realize that time has stopped for us forever now.

There is no more screaming and sobbing, just silent despair that is really the sound of light and life fading away. They didn't just take you, they took us all.

I look at that beautiful face, stuck in that nightmare, and I see something that in all the sixteen years of knowing you I never saw before. I see hundreds and hundreds of freckles. The paleness of your face added to the harsh, bright lights has highlighted them and they are the one bit of colour I can find on you. I fixate on them and as I try to count them all, I start to pray. Maybe if I count every single one, God will let you come home. Like a sick game, I play it again and again, but my mind is muddled and I have forgotten what order numbers go in and so, in the end, I give up and I try to kiss every one instead.

This will be what I remember for the rest of my life. This is what I will take from this horrible place, this horrific day – not the cold, not the yellow, not the wires, but your freckles. Every single one. This will be our code so that when you decide to come back to me, I will know it's really you.

Freckle, Freckle, Kiss, Kiss.

My brother Ben was murdered on 29 June 2008. I have used a lot of words in connection with my brother over the years – annoying, lazy, 'go shop please' – but never, ever did I think I would speak his name next to a terrible word like that. Sixteen-year-olds shouldn't be linked with the word 'murder' because they should have all the time left in the world.

He died on the day that I was supposed to be moving

out. I was the one who was meant to be leaving. I had spent twenty-five years wrapped up in the soft, comfy cotton wool of family in a house that was filled with noise and laughter, love and affection. It's not a cliché, I promise. It's not to get more sympathy – to pretend that everything was so perfect that his death hurt us that much more – it's just the truth. We were just lucky.

I didn't want to leave home. In my house, there was always somebody there, whether you needed to laugh or cry, or shout or scream. I didn't want to leave my mum's cooking or my dad's moaning or my sisters who stole my make-up but who had twice as much to steal back. I didn't want to leave my brother, because then who would sneak into my room at midnight to watch *Friends* or scary films that would have us both wide awake until morning, telling each other jokes to chase the horrors away?

Friends told me it would be exciting – no rules, my own space, house parties. My mum told me it was worth a try and I could come back whenever I wanted, and my dad told me it might finally teach me how to cook and wash up. I told myself I was twenty-five and it was time to grow up, but I was dreading it. I couldn't bear the thought of not seeing every member of my family at least once a day, every day – how bittersweet and ironic that seems now.

I went to my new flat that Saturday morning, prepared to clean and dust and make it my own. Unfortunately (or fortunately as I would decide later) I was locked out and unable to get in. At a loss, I decided to go shopping and buy myself some moving-in presents, as surely that was the best thing about getting your own flat? I bought mannequins and cushions, chandeliers and candles. I tried to compensate for the lack of people in my new flat by filling it with as much glamour and glitz as possible.

My spending spree led me outside the shop where Ben worked. Sixteen years old and he was already a grafter – not that my parents were the child-labour type. My brother had been working since he was nine years old of his own free will: first making a quick pound doing chores for us all, then upping the game to a fiver each time when he grew wiser, before moving on to market stalls, sausage factories and, finally, his dream job as an IT assistant in an Internet café. Ben knew what he wanted and he did his best to get it. Knocking on the door of the café every day after his first interview, asking if they'd found anybody yet, assuring them he would work really, really hard – I think they gave him the job just to shut him up, but they knew they were on to a good thing.

He only had one mishap while he was there – in his first month, he called my mum in a panic because he'd stupidly locked up the shop and left the keys inside with all the windows wide open. He'd tried to borrow a ladder from the local Sainsbury's to break back in but when that didn't work, he called the one person who could always resolve a crisis – our mum. He was almost in tears and was so worried he would lose the job he'd worked so hard for. Mum, feeling sorry for him, called up his boss and apologized profusely on his behalf before driving him round to pick up some spare keys. As well as saving his skin, she was also conned out of a tenner by him playing the sympathy card, but he learned his lesson from that experience and worked as hard as he'd promised, which led to him being promoted to Graphics Designer in his first month. Sixteen and he had already fulfilled one of his dreams – I thank God for that every day now.

Standing outside his shop holding all my new belongings, I debated whether to go in and visit him. Although he'd been there a couple of months, I didn't usually disturb him at work, but thought it would be funny to watch him being all grown-up. My bags were heavy, though, and I had work pretty soon and didn't know whether I could spare the time. I now look on the decision to go in and see him as the best one I have ever made and probably ever will make in my entire life. Ten minutes to spare going in to see my brother meant ten more minutes that I would have never had had with him – it was also the last ten minutes I ever spent with him.

I bought him some food from McDonald's as I knew he'd be starving and went in to show him my new stuff – he laughed and said it was stupid and girly. He showed me photos on his phone of a cute baby he knew – I laughed and said he was gay and girly. He ate the McDonald's in two bites and gave me such a grateful look you'd have thought I'd given him a diamond Xbox. Our time together was interrupted by customer after customer but I was so proud when I saw how mature and helpful he was with them all.

I decided to leave him in peace and gave him a kiss, which he quickly wiped off and followed up with a dirty look for embarrassing him in his place of business. He said he'd see me later and I said bye and walked away.

I said bye and walked away.

It was my brother's last day on this earth; it was the last time I would ever see him alive, be able to talk to him or see him smile at me and, after ten minutes, I said bye and walked away.

That decision is the worst I ever made and probably ever will make in my entire life.

The rest of that day is a blur – whether because everything was erased by what happened later or because the only important part of that day was the time spent with my brother, I'm not sure – but here's what I do remember.

I went to work – I was doing a play in Hackney at the time and it was our second night of performances. I was petrified and nervous but it was a good show and I was happy. I walked off stage smiling and proud. I turned down offers of celebratory drinks, which was highly unusual for me, because I was simply shattered after the adrenalin rush of the show. In hindsight, another good decision.

I got home to find the house empty, bar my stepbrother, Christopher. My mum, dad and youngest sister, Georgia, had gone away for the weekend, my other sister Jade was out partying and Ben had come home from work and gone straight out to meet his friends. I asked Christopher which friends he'd gone out with but he didn't know. This wasn't strange as he didn't live with us and so wouldn't know which friends of Ben's were with him, but what was strange was that he said nobody had come to collect Ben – he'd gone out on his own.

This wasn't like my brother – wherever he went he had one of his best friends tagging along, to the point where it often felt like I had four or five younger brothers. They went everywhere together and for Ben to have left the house on a Saturday night without having one of his mates there to check that his hair looked good was very odd. I thought about calling him to check he was OK but decided he'd probably only gone round to a friend's house and it was best not to disturb him. In hindsight, another bad decision.

I remember making some spaghetti bolognese for him to eat when he came in and then getting annoyed because I knew he didn't eat mince and now he wouldn't have any dinner. Since Ben was little, he had 'hated' red meat. He would turn his nose up at a steak or the lovely piece of beef my mum would do for a Sunday roast but would scoff down a hamburger or two in seconds. This fake vegetarianism made me laugh but drove my mum crazy. I decided that the McDonald's I'd bought him a few hours before made up for my lack of culinary skills and, because I was so tired, said goodnight to Christopher and went to bed early.

OK, I lied before. The worst decision I ever made wasn't walking away from my brother hours earlier, or not calling to check on him when I got home – it was turning my phone to silent when I went to bed that night.

My stomach rolls over even writing those words and the guilt I feel at what I did will never, ever leave me. I have never told anybody, not even my parents, but there it is – my shameful secret and the reason I partly blame myself for my brother's death. That night, I was so tired and so reluctant to be disturbed by drunken texts and calls from friends that I figured it would be OK to put my phone on silent.

And that's when the nightmare started.

What had been a normal day should have ended with a normal night's sleep and me waking to have breakfast with my family. Instead it ended with my family being one down and me never waking up properly again.

The house phone rang at half-two on the morning of Sunday, 29 June. Anybody who hears their phone ring at that time knows it's not good and I was no exception. I stumbled over to pick it up, half asleep and half in fear.

'Brooke,' said my sister Jade. 'Something's happened to Ben.'

'What?' I whispered.

The sound of sobbing. 'He's been stabbed.'

Three words that can change your life. Three men that use a knife. It doesn't seem fair – there shouldn't be enough power behind simple words or simple men to take away a force, a personality like Ben, but apparently there is. I remember screaming for Christopher to call a taxi, I tried to get dressed but couldn't remember how to and then I was outside my house, kneeling in the middle of the road, crying and praying – for the taxi to hurry up, for it to all be a big mistake, for my brother to be OK if it wasn't.

When you're the oldest sibling, you have a certain amount of responsibility – in fact, apart from your parents, you have all the responsibility. That's the rules. I loved being the oldest sister – I loved bossing everybody around, always getting the front seat in the car, never having to wear hand-me-downs and playing the 'I'm the oldest so I'm in charge' card. They are an older sibling's rights and it's what anyone who is one does.

But should an older sibling have to make a phone call to her parents that she knows will destroy them forever? Should she have to make that choice between calling them for help or hoping that she can deal with it on her own (and that by the time they find out he will be home and smiling and saying it's just a scratch)? Should she have to listen to her mum screaming after she's been snatched from sleep and told something bad has happened to her only son? It wasn't fair. I didn't want to be the oldest any more.

Christopher and I got to the hospital at three o'clock after waiting an eternity for the taxi, who then still charged me the full fare. I remember counting out my pennies, wasting precious seconds – furious that he was charging me when he knew what had happened to my brother and amazed that my scrambled brain had remembered to bring money out at all. We ran into the hospital that for some reason was deathly quiet and Jade fell on me, sobbing. I begged her for news or information but she knew nothing. A friend who'd been at the scene had called her and told her Ben had been stabbed and she'd rushed straight to him, detouring to a wrong hospital on the way, losing her precious time. Nobody had told her anything yet.

After a few minutes when we all just looked at each other in shock, a nurse came in and asked who was in charge. My mouth wouldn't open. I didn't want to say me because with that answer came responsibilities and decisions, but my parents were rushing along a motorway, desperately trying to get to Ben, and there was no one else to step up.

After learning that I was the eldest, she looked at me with a kindness and sympathy that didn't disguise the seriousness in her eyes and told me that Ben had been brought in a while ago with a stab wound to his stomach, two to his lungs and one in his chest that had given him a hole in his heart. He had lost a great deal of blood, he was in surgery and he was critical.

Funnily enough, that word didn't scare me, because when I watched those doctor programmes and they said someone was critical, it was never as bad as it seemed and they always made it through. I figured she just didn't want to give us false hope and, as she assured us they were doing all they could and rushed back to help them save my brother, I really believed he was going to be OK.

Nobody likes waiting in hospital – the smell, the chaos, the feeling that something bad is happening somewhere in a room above you. Waiting in hospital to find out if a loved one is going to live is what I would imagine hell to be like. We couldn't speak, we couldn't move, time dragged by with seconds feeling like hours and all we could do was listen for the footsteps that we hoped would bring us good news.

My parents got to the hospital at half-four. By then, my boyfriend Ray had arrived and was holding my hand tightly in shock, accompanying me to the bathroom every time I needed to vomit and handing out cups of tea that we sipped at like a lifeline. I will never, ever, forget my parents' faces when they first walked into that hospital. They looked as if they had aged a hundred years in an hour. My fourteen-year-old sister Georgia, Ben's best friend and mortal enemy rolled into one, looked heartbroken and I knew at that moment that even if Ben made it through this, we would never be the same again. One of us had been hurt and we would never forget the pain that had been caused.

Again, it is blurry. Policemen came in and asked questions. The nurse came back in and updated my parents. She told us that they had sewed up the hole in Ben's heart and pumped him full of new blood and that after they had wrapped up surgery, they would be transferring him to intensive care, where we could all go and be with him and encourage him to pull through.

At that point, the head surgeon, the hands that had worked on my baby brother, came into the room to talk to us. He didn't look like a surgeon – he was wearing a smart suit and had greying hair – in fact, he looked more like a headmaster. I checked him everywhere for signs of Ben's blood but could see none – I suppose they are very careful not to upset anybody. He shook my mum and dad's hands and it struck me that those hands and this man had touched Ben in places my parents never had – at least physically – and that felt wrong. I didn't want the last touch on Ben to be that of a stranger.

The surgeon reiterated what the nurse had said. Ben was critical but still here. Surgery was finished – they had done all they could. Now it was our turn to cheer him on and convince him not to leave us. They told us he had lost thirty pints of blood. The average young boy's body holds seven. He lost all his blood four times over. The surgeon asked us about Ben – what he was like, what his hobbies were, what he wanted to be when he grew up. Speaking about his future made me believe he was definitely coming home. All that personality and potential couldn't just be erased. The surgeon shook our hands and we thanked him with all our hearts and as he left somebody asked him what the chances of Ben surviving were.

'Fifty–fifty,' he replied.

Those odds were scary but reassuring. He had as much chance of coming home as not. I could believe in those odds; I would definitely bet on them. Ben would be OK, we all told each other. He had to pull through – he still owed me twenty pounds.

While we waited for the nurse to take my parents to his bedside, I debated whether to go to the hospital chapel and beg God for mercy. We weren't a particularly religious family – I only spoke to God when I wanted something and I know that's terrible but I figured in those circumstances we had to try everything. I was scared to leave, though. I worried that the second I walked away something would happen and I didn't want to miss it, good or bad.

In the end, Ray took me to pray and I knelt in a tiny little hospital room that wasn't a church at all apart from in name, and I spoke to God. I felt Him, I cried to Him, I offered my eternal services if He would just let my brother come home. I told Him that Ben was too good, too special to die, but then seeing as He had created him, He should have known that anyway. I left feeling slightly better, convinced that God had heard me and would help.

I got back just as my parents were going in to see Ben. I was so scared for them – what would he look like? How could they face seeing their little boy so hurt? No matter what, though, I knew the second Ben saw them he would be fine – whether they bribed him with presents or threatened him with being grounded, they would make him pull through.

Literally five minutes after they left, they were back. Apparently Ben's kidneys had begun to worsen and the medical staff had to do some things to stabilize him. This didn't sound good but we didn't panic. The doctors didn't look too worried. He was in the best hands. He hadn't seen my mum and dad yet, so of course he couldn't start to get strong.

Ten minutes later they were back with the words that will haunt us forever:

'We're really sorry but we think he is going to die. You'd better come.'

I remember every one of us in that room screamed. I remember half of us sinking to the floor, our legs unable to hold the weight and grief any more and half of us lashing out at whatever was near, kicking walls and tables in anger and fury. My mum and dad were rushed to Ben and the rest of us descended into complete silence. Like a demented moron, I began to babble: 'Everyone, let's pray! If we just pray he'll be fine, I promise you . . . Hold hands, all together . . . Please God, make him OK, please God, make him OK . . .' Nobody joined in – they weren't as stupid as me.

What seemed an eternity later – but was actually only ten minutes – the nurse walked in and by the look on her face we all knew. But nobody asked the question because if we asked we would get a definite answer and at this point there was still hope. At this point, I could still have a brother.

———————

But somebody had to ask. Someone had to take responsibility and, as my parents weren't in the room, again it came down to me.

'Is he gone?'

'Yes, I'm sorry.'

Again there was screaming and kicking and cursing and complete disbelief. How could Ben, a sixteen-year-old clown, a boy with a smile that could melt you and a laugh that was completely contagious, be gone? How could Ben's heart, a heart that was so big even the largest hole would be unable to hurt it, have stopped beating? How could he have been 50 per cent coming home half an hour ago and now 100 per cent not?

It felt like I had died myself. I couldn't breathe, I couldn't move, I couldn't understand. How could my brother have simply gone out and not come back again? What had happened today? What had happened to God?

When we had calmed down enough, which took a long time, especially for my sister Jade, who couldn't control her anger and horror, they told us we could go and see him. For me, this was too late, as I was sure that if they had let us see him hours before then there was no way he would have left us. If they had just let one of us give him a kiss, he would have known that he was not alone and that we were all out there fighting for him, and he would have made it. Already the thoughts and obsessions and what-ifs were driving me crazy.

The nurse told us that our parents were 'sorting things

———————

out', and so she led us, Ben's brother and sisters, big and little, to a cubicle that was curtained off. It looked like any normal cubicle, a place I had seen various friends and relatives in, a place I had been in myself. It certainly didn't look like a place you could die in.

But when we stepped through the curtain there was no mistake and it finally, finally hit me. Up until now, I was kidding myself. We hadn't seen Ben, so how could they be sure it was my brother? How did we know they hadn't confused him with some other boy whose family would have to go through all this heartbreak while we rejoiced in the error? What if there were two boys who had been stabbed that night and this other one had died and Ben was still upstairs recovering, waiting for us to go and collect him?

But there was only one boy, and it was definitely my brother and he was definitely dead. Nothing could have prepared me for the change death brings to a person, even within five minutes. No words can describe the horror of looking at someone you love so much and not recognizing them, but I will do my best.

Ben was obviously gone and in his place was a cold, hard, yellow shell with an expression on his face that showed many things. Anger, upset, pain – emotions that we were lucky enough not to have seen much on his face in his poor, short life.

Once our eyes got over the shocking colour of his skin and the coldness of his body, we began to recognize him, which I think made things even worse. While he was a stranger it was easier not to hurt, but once we saw parts of Ben in this damaged and broken body, the pain became unbearable. The one thing I thank God for now is that all the parts that made Ben what he was were not harmed. Miraculously, there wasn't a scratch on his beautiful face, for if there had been, I think my heart would have stopped right then and there. The parts that obviously were hurt were covered up and this made it seem strange and unreal, as if we had just stumbled in on him sleeping. You could convince yourself of this if it were not for the pain in his face. It killed me that this would be the way he was immortalized. For a boy who laughed and winked so much, he would not have wanted to be stuck this way.

They tell you to take as long as you need but there is not enough time in the world. When you know it is the last time you are going to see somebody, how can you walk away? At that point, we didn't know about funeral homes and morgues, we had never had to deal with anything like this. For us, this was the last time we would ever see Ben and we couldn't possibly leave him.

My mum and dad came in and we all stood crowded round, touching him where we could. My mum rubbed his feet and hands to warm them up, I blew on his freckly nose to help and everybody else just stroked and kissed him, trying to absorb as much Ben as they could. You would think that the thought of touching a dead body would be repulsive, but not when it's one of your own. If

I could, I would have taken his body home and hugged it every second I could – rather that than nothing at all.

Finally, we could do no more. Nothing was going to change. A miracle wasn't going to happen with Ben suddenly opening his eyes and saying, 'Ha ha, fooled you!' It was time to leave him.

We walked out of that hospital broken. Each of us destroyed and shattered, both mentally and physically. All we wanted was to lie down and sleep forever, to join Ben, but there was too much to do. Phone calls to be made – every one of them heartbreaking as we told the story over and over again, each time as unbelievable as the last. Forms to be filled in, plans to be made, questions to be asked. And there were many. Up until now, we had had no time to wonder about the events that had led us here, had led to my brother being stolen from us, had led to our family being ripped apart. But now, with life without Ben stretching into eternity, there was plenty of time to wonder what the hell had happened that night. And with questions came answers, and with answers came anger and consequences.

Chapter 2

I wander around the house looking for you. There are reminders of you everywhere, in every room and every passage, but these aren't good enough. I want you. It's like when we were all younger and would play hide and seek, splitting up into two teams. You were always the last to be found, preferring to hide for hours in a cramped space just to jump out and scare one of us, long after we had forgotten we were playing. I think you must be playing a game with me and just need to be found.

I start in the kitchen, as this is where I am most likely to find you — raiding the cupboard for every last biscuit or sweet, or cooking amazing meals made up in your head then leaving every burned pot and pan for someone else to clean. I look but you aren't there. I even look in the cupboards and the fridge, just in case, and laugh at my silliness, but I never know when it comes to you.

Next, I try the living room, where only the night before you died we watched **Big Brother***, both of us curled up on the couch* *as we cried with laughter. I check both couches in case you're fast asleep after a hard day at school, tie loosened, forehead uncreased, smiling peacefully. But the living room is silent and empty with only a Ben-shaped dent in the cushions to remind me.*

I continue up the stairs and check the bathroom – you're always in there hogging the shower while I bang on the door and demand to be let in. But the shower is silent and I don't hear your voice shouting back, 'Five more minutes!'

I go up to your room. You were so excited to finally get your own room last year. You spent weeks and weeks making it your own – painting beautiful art and graffiti on every space you could, getting into so much trouble along the way. Posters of Lucy Pinder, your ideal girl, are stuck on the door. Photos of you and your friends and family are pinned up on every wall. It's like a twisted funhouse at the fair – I see you looking back at me from every angle yet I can't see the real you. Your Guitar Hero is lying on the floor – only a few days ago you taught me how to play it and had to admit that I was 'not bad for a girl'.

Your schoolbooks are in a pile in the corner. A cruel reminder that you had only just finished school and were so excited to be starting the next chapter of your life. If you could talk to me, I know you'd be trying to make a joke, laughing that it might have at least happened a week before so you could've got out of your exams. I still don't understand why you can't talk to me. I call your mobile and get your voicemail – 'This is Ben, the buff one, Kinsella. Please leave a message.' I do. I tell you to come home. You will get this and be worried you are late or in trouble and rush through the door any minute now. I go down to meet you.

Why Ben?

I check the other rooms on my way just in case. They are empty too.

I finish up in my room, as you're always in here, giving your sisters advice on men, curled up on the end of my bed watching TV, driving us mad to borrow a pound. All these lovely memories are here but so is another – I remember a phone call, Jade saying you were hurt, a voice saying you had died. But this is silly. Of course this didn't happen because I've just seen proof everywhere that you live. You'll walk in the door any minute, shouting that you're starving, smiling at me as you pass, letting me know this is all just a bad dream. Or you'll jump out from where you're hiding, laughing loudly, and the game will be over. To keep you happy, I go down to the beginning of the house and start my search again, trying harder this time. I know you are here, I just have to find you.

You know that feeling when you wake from a nightmare? That blessed, sweet feeling of knowing that it's not as scary as you thought, nothing bad has actually happened and everything is just as you left it when you closed your eyes? I used to love that feeling when I was younger – I'd wake up, safe in my own bed, relieved there were no monsters and baddies out there and happily get on with my day.

The first time I woke up after my brother died, that was the best feeling I'd ever known in my life. I started breathing again, I started laughing at the silliness of myself, I got up to shake off the horrors and reassure myself that I still had a little brother – and then I turned and saw Ray lying next to me, and from the devastated look in his eyes I knew the nightmare had only just begun. My bed would never feel safe again – it was the place where I'd received the phone call that Ben had been hurt, where I'd realized that monsters and baddies did exist – they had taken my brother from me and I would never, ever have a happy day again.

When we arrived back from the hospital on that fateful Sunday, my sisters and I went straight to Ben's room to soak up whatever he had left there before he went out the previous night. As always, it looked like a bomb had hit it. Clothes, pants and socks were everywhere – he had obviously tried on every outfit he owned, wanting to look his best, no doubt having certain ladies to impress. The smell of his teenage aftershave and hair gel was heavy in the air and beneath that, only if you were his family and knew where to look, was the essence of Ben. That wonderful smell that only one of us could have picked out from a crowd of hundreds – the smell that was already beginning to fade and soon would only be in our memories . . . and maybe not for long even there.

We each picked an item to cling on to. Jade put on his clothes – something he would have definitely moaned about had he still had a voice, for nobody touched his precious designer jumpers that he worked so hard for. Georgia buried her head in his pillow and cried herself to sleep – fourteen years old and exhausted, unable to understand why her big brother and protector was gone. And I chose a sock. A stinky, sticky sock that was the strongest Ben-smelling thing I could find.

I wore it like a glove puppet, constantly rubbing it like a charm, wishing it would bring him back. If I woke in the night and couldn't find it, I cried until it was back safely on my hand. I probably cried more for that stupid sock in those first few days than I did for its owner.

My mum and dad became the great parents they are. Trying to make us eat, stop us falling apart, worrying about the kids they had left. The house was too quiet without Ben in it. Everything was different; it was like we were in a stranger's house. His things were everywhere and we tiptoed around them silently, scared to move them in case he came back looking for them.

The news broke fast. We didn't even have to tell anyone apart from close family because with me being in the public eye as an actress, the media had picked up on Ben's death immediately. How, I don't know – it all happened so quickly, one minute he was here, then he was gone and suddenly he was headline news.

Ex-Eastenders star's brother stabbed to death
17th teenager dies in London this year

Because of the horrific amount of stabbings that had been happening recently, and because my brother had happened to have a semi-famous sister, everybody wanted a piece of him. Every news channel ran his story and it was so strange to see his beautiful face on TV – we always knew the world would know his name but we never imagined it would be like this. Then the tidal wave began. Phones ringing, doorbells chiming, people asking the same two horrific questions. The first was 'Is it true?' and every time we had to say yes, it broke our hearts again because we so wanted to give a different answer. The second question was much harder: 'What happened?' We didn't know. Nobody had told us.

The police came to the house the day that he died to update us on the enquiry. It was surreal as none of us had had to deal with the police before and suddenly they were there in our kitchen, scary and official, while we sat stiffly, petrified they were going to blame us in some way. They told us what little they knew. Ben had gone to a local pub called Shillibeers that night. Ironically, it was a pub where only a few years before I had thrown my twenty-first birthday party, a quiet little place where I spent my special day with friends and family, and even managed to get my then-twelve-year-old brother to allow me a dance, something that had grown impossible over the past couple of years. I couldn't believe that a place which held such great memories for me was now the scene of my brother's death. He went to the pub that night with some friends that none of us really knew. It wasn't his usual crowd or anybody that he'd ever really spoken of before. The pub wasn't a normal haunt of his – he hadn't been back there since my birthday. He had gone there for a number of reasons, we heard – to celebrate the end of his GCSE exams, because a popular DJ that he loved was playing at the venue, because a girl he liked was going to be there . . . they all made sense but they weren't good enough reasons to die.

There had been a big fight inside the pub at some point. Ben was in no way involved. This much the police were sure of and so were we. Ben was not that type of boy. He didn't get into fights – he didn't know how to after growing up with three sisters. The fight was between two different groups of boys and it spilled out on to the street. Most people in the pub had run out to see what was going on and if any of their friends were involved. The police believed my brother could have been one of these people.

Later I heard that, as it was near the end of the night, and the bouncers didn't want the fight to escalate, they closed the gates on everyone outside. I don't want to blame anybody for my brother's death apart from those who held the knife but this horrified me. Fair enough if you're dealing with a crowd of angry grown men, but a group of teenage boys? What are bouncers for if not to deal with situations like this?

After being locked out, my brother began to make his way home, walking up the road with a few other boys – apparently he was last in the group, stuck at the back. Whether these boys were involved in the original fight was unclear but one of them looked back and realized they were being chased. They all began to run, up a long road and around a corner. At some point, my brother had given up running – maybe because he was out of breath, maybe because his feet were hurting and he couldn't run any more, but probably because he thought he didn't have to run. He hadn't done anything wrong that night so why should he run away? For some unknown reason, he crossed over to the other side of the road – we now believe he was just getting out of the way. If all the trouble was heading in one direction, wasn't it best to head in another? This makes sense, but it was this sense that got him killed. Whoever was chasing the boys saw my brother as the easier target. They followed him instead, caught him behind a van and stabbed him over and over again. Then they left him on the pavement to die.

Amazingly, but what breaks my shattered heart all over again, my brother then found the strength to stand up from this horrific attack and walk around the corner, where people had begun to come back, having realized something was not right.

What followed was the usual procedure – people began to scream and panic and ambulances and the police were called. A friend of Ben's was one of the first to reach him and held him as he lay on the pavement, trying his hardest to stop the blood seeping from him. Two other boys who were simply visiting London also stopped and began to give him first aid but despite trying their hardest, they couldn't do much.

Why Ben?

The first thing I asked of these people who were with Ben at this time was whether he was conscious or not. I wanted to know if he knew what had happened to him, if he was suffering, if he was scared? I was told that he was awake and was whispering things nobody could understand, but that he didn't look in pain and kept trying to drift off to sleep. The only coherent words he said were 'I've been stabbed', which answered my first and most important question. I was hoping with all my heart that he had been so shocked that he wouldn't have known the evil that had befallen him. I'd read that when you're stabbed it just feels like a punch and I clung on to the hope that my brother would have fallen asleep before he knew the truth, but, unfortunately, he knew from the second they did it.

From there, Ben went into the ambulance and on to hospital. We later found out that his heart had actually stopped there on that cold pavement, but that he had fought and come back, only for it to stop again on the way and then one last final time. Three times was the charm for my brother. Again, we begged for any words anyone had heard him speak – any kind of message that we could cling on to. The only words he uttered were 'I'm cold' and 'I can't breathe'.

This was the story we were given, the reason behind his murder, the reason he would never come home. It was early days and the police were still trying to piece everything together but there were so many gaps and questions unanswered that we couldn't make sense of it. We knew nothing would ever make sense of it, but it just seemed so surreal and unbelievable. For a start, where were all the other people who'd been kicked out of the pub? Had there been no one on that street at all, no one to help him, or had people just been too scared? Why him? The police said he hadn't been involved in any fight – they knew that for certain – so why did they pick on him? Was it mistaken identity or just a case of 'we'll take whoever we can'?

The police left us with all these questions, but promised they would work their hardest to answer them. They needed all the help they could get and were asking people to come forward as witnesses but, at this time, there was nothing more to say.

For us there was plenty to say. We wanted and needed to know more – why had he chosen to walk that way when, in fact, he lived in the opposite direction? Why had he left with that particular group of boys who weren't even good friends of his and, most importantly, why had he stopped running? Unfortunately, these were questions that could probably only be answered by Ben himself and he wasn't here to tell us. We needed to know if he had suffered, and how had he suffered? Did he know we were there with him at the end?

I also wanted to know more morbid things. I wanted to know exactly how many wounds he had and where they were, because only when I knew this could I stop making up the worst things in my head. I wanted to know if they had just stabbed him or did they beat him up or kick him and hurt him even more? I wanted to know if he had seen the knife and how big it was and had he been frozen with fear or had he been brave and shouted at them and tried to fight back? Not that he had a chance when there were many of them and only one of him, but knowing my brother, he would have tried his best. I needed to know these things, horrific as it sounds. I needed to know how badly they had hurt my baby brother so I knew what I was dealing with.

We also needed to know where Ben was. It felt so strange and my heart hurt for my mum and dad, as in all the sixteen years of his life, they had always known where he was. They knew where all of us were. They were the best parents you could ask for and were fair but firm, which is why if we were going out, we didn't sneak around and lie.

I had learned my lesson years ago when, at the age of fifteen, a next-door neighbour had invited me to go round to her friend's house where a group of cute boys would be. Afraid my parents might say no, I pretended I was staying at this girl's house and would be in all night watching videos. I forgot how easy it would be for my mum to check up on me if I was meant to be staying next door, which of course she did. When she rang my mobile to see where I was, I made out I had gone into the West End to a pizza restaurant and naturally she didn't believe me and ordered me home immediately. When I got in, I was scrutinized and interrogated on my whereabouts that evening. Having been acting for years I thought I could convince them easily and gave an Oscar-winning performance that I had simply gone into town for pizza. Unfortunately, I forgot the drawbacks of having a London taxi driver as a dad and when he began quizzing me on every route I had taken to get there and back, and asked me exactly which street the restaurant I had gone to was on, I knew the game was up. I was caught out lying, promptly grounded and from then on I never hid where I was going again. I passed this lesson on to my younger siblings, which is why we always told our parents where we were going and asked for permission first – that way, they could keep tabs on us and check we were safe.

Now, after keeping Ben safe for sixteen years, through no fault of their own they had lost him, and had no idea where he was.

The most awful thing was that on the night he died, for the first time ever, they didn't even know he'd gone out. They had gone down to our family chalet on the coast for the weekend, something they often did, taking Georgia with them. Jade and I were obviously old enough to be left home alone but Ben had only just been allowed to stay home at the weekends, not particularly because they felt that at sixteen he was old enough but because he had just got his job, which meant he had to work weekends. Because it meant so much to him, he was allowed to stay at home with me and Jade, providing he behaved.

Before they left that weekend, they had a small row with Ben and lectured him for not walking the dog, not tidying up, being lazy – things every parent must argue with their children about on a daily basis. They left not really on speaking terms with him – something my mum will never forgive herself for. Usually, she would have kissed him goodbye and smiled cheerfully, but this time she was annoyed with him and had every right to be. How was she to know she wouldn't ever get another chance to kiss him? How was she to know that her firm words would be the last she ever said to her son? I tried to tell her it wasn't her fault, that she was only being a normal mum, and that actually he had come straight upstairs and laughed to his sisters about our parents driving him mad, but she wouldn't be consoled and I couldn't blame her. Just as I would carry my guilt over turning my phone off, so would she about this.

Sadly, because he was at work all the next day until late, she didn't get to speak to him on the Saturday. He spoke to my sister Jade and told her he was going to come and meet her, and she relayed this message to my mum, who told me, and we were all happy. We knew where he was, he would be with one of us – there was no need to worry. But he never turned up to meet my sister. He went to play football around the corner from our house and that was the last we knew until it was too late.

I know what people will think, and have actually said – that it was our fault for not looking after him. That it was my parents' fault for letting him go out to a pub that night.

'What's a sixteen-year-old doing in a pub anyway? He deserves to die.'

I don't want to give credit to the person who left that lovely message on a tribute site set up for Ben but it shows the mentality of some people. And it voiced my parent's worst nightmares. No, they hadn't known Ben had gone to a pub that night but if, under normal circumstances, he had asked them, they probably would have said yes. After checking where it was and who was going, they would have preferred him to go somewhere they believed was safe and policed, rather than hang about on the streets where kids are prone to get into trouble. Add to that he had finished his exams and wanted to celebrate, that almost everybody in there was of a similar age to him and that my brother was a good kid who wouldn't get steaming drunk and cause trouble, I think any logical person will conclude that it's not my parents' fault. However, my parents can't look at this logically. They only see that their son is dead and that for this one time they couldn't keep him safe and this will haunt them forever. As if they didn't have enough to go through, the added guilt hurts them even more.

Although we didn't know where our real Ben was, his body was being stored in a fridge waiting to go over to the coroners', where they would carry out all sorts of tests and make all kinds of reports, all resulting in the same thing – this boy is dead.

I couldn't bear the thought of his little body naked in a fridge. When you see or hear of death on the news or TV, it's sad but you don't think of these little details. They are insignificant, except when you're talking about somebody you love. Then they matter. I rambled on and on about rescue plans, wanting to break in and steal him back, and people listened to me indulgently, thinking I was talking in grief when really I was completely serious. They managed to calm me by telling me that we could go and see Ben the next day. In my head, if I could still see Ben, he was still here and there was a chance I could wake him up. I prayed for tomorrow to come sooner.

That first day, we did what many people who are grieving do – we went and got drunk. It started with just close family and friends congregating in a pub round the corner from my house, crying and telling stories, each person trying to bring him back with their memories. Slowly, as word spread, more and more people joined us until we took up two pubs and spilled out on to the street – most people holding a Magners or a cherry beer, which was Ben's favourite drink. All his friends were there, sobbing, disbelieving, and hugging and comforting them made me feel better, as if I was hugging my own brother and wiping his tears away.

Eventually, after too many brandies and no food for two

days, I made my way home and up into Ben's bed. I couldn't bring myself to sleep in my own bed again, as I couldn't get the memory of that phone call out of my head, and so I lay in my brother's bed, feeling his fading warmth, and waited for tomorrow when I would see him again.

The next day, my parents and I went to the morgue to see Ben. They wanted to see what he looked like before my younger sisters saw him and I decided I didn't care how bad he looked, he was still my brother and I wanted to see him regardless. We got there and met the coroner, who answered a few questions for us. He told us that my brother hadn't suffered much and that they hadn't beaten him up before stabbing him – answers I should have been happy with but somehow found hard to believe. How can you not suffer when being stabbed? A paper cut hurts enough, let alone anything worse. After filling in official forms and signing death certificates, he led us into a view-ing room to see Ben and told us that because of the ongoing investigation, we would be unable to touch him. This really hurt. How could I wake him up if I couldn't touch him? To get Ben up for school my mum would have to practically pull him out of bed and when all I wanted to do was kiss him, not touching would be unbearable.

Thankfully, Ben looked better than he had a couple of days before in the hospital. He'd lost that yellow colour and without all the drips and machines, he looked like he was getting better. It didn't make sense. What hadn't changed though was that awful expression on his face of hurt and confusion and it struck me again that this was the face he would carry with him for eternity. They had covered him in a velvet sheet of purple and gold – his favourite colours. We hadn't asked for this but he'd been given it and he looked like a little prince.

We sat behind the glass for a long time, talking nonsense and trying to press as close to him as we could through the barrier. It was almost as if he was in a coma and we were trying to wake him up by reminding him of normal things. 'Nanny said to tell you this and you won't believe it, this happened . . .' In my mind, he was just in a deep sleep and all I had to do was find the right key to unlock him and bring him home. This state of denial would go on for a long time – maybe in some ways it will never go away – but in those early days it was the only thing keeping me sane and for that I was grateful. We weren't allowed much time as the coroner said it wasn't a good idea to keep a body out for too long, especially in midsummer – another reminder that Ben was now just a body. We left with promises to come back tomorrow and went home to find that in our absence, the police had made a breakthrough in the case.

In the early hours after Ben's death, the police had arrested a couple of boys in connection with his murder, although it turned out they had been friends of Ben's and were completely innocent. By the next day, though, they knew who they were really looking for and who they believed was responsible – something that amazed me. I don't know if it was just them doing their job well, or if people had come forward to help, but they seemed to know from the beginning who might have killed my brother. The names meant nothing to me or my family – they were three strangers who had just come along and ruined our lives – but once I knew them, they kept going round and round in my head like an annoying song you can't shake off. Unfortunately, they had gone to ground, something that, for me, demonstrated their guilt, and at first the police hadn't been able to locate them. Now though, they had managed to find two of them and had arrested them after they'd tried to escape through the window of the house they were hiding in. They were being interviewed as we spoke.

Although it was good news, and we were glad they were in custody, the police told us that there still wasn't sufficient evidence to charge them. Despite news reports, they had found no weapons and could only hold them for a certain amount of time before they had to let them go. This news devastated us. We didn't know for certain if the arrested boys had killed my brother, but the police seemed to think so and to let them walk away would finish us off. Finally, the police asked us if we would all be prepared to come and do a press conference and ask the public to come forward and help in any way they could. We debated long and hard about this – we'd do anything to help get justice for Ben, but it was still so raw for us. We were constantly crying, we were still in shock and to go and face the nation like this terrified us. I was used to speaking publicly as I'd been in the entertainment industry all my life, but the rest of my family hated it. My mum usually ran a mile from a camera and to have all eyes pointed at her at this terrible time scared the life out of her. But there was never really a question as to if we would do it.

Together we came up with a statement to read about Ben. It was so hard. We had one chance to put into words the way we felt about Ben, one chance to persuade anybody who knew anything to come forward, to make them care enough to help. At the same time, we begged the teenagers of our country to stop carrying and using knives, to stop ripping apart loving families like ours.

The police took us all – Mum, Dad, me, Jade and Georgia – to a police station. There, every news channel was waiting for us, ready to show our grief to the world. I was elected spokesperson and, as we sat at a long table holding hands to face the media, we begged and pleaded for somebody to help us. We then went home for an agonizing wait.

To everybody's surprise, something worked. I don't know if somebody came forward or if the police simply found more evidence but that evening, a couple of hours before the deadline was up and they were due to let the suspects go, the head detective came round and said that they now had enough to charge the two men, Michael Alleyne and Juress Kika. On top of that, a third man, Jade Braithwaite, had handed himself into a police station that day in connection with the murder of my brother.

We wept with relief and half-celebrated (there would never be a proper celebration for us again) and I even went to the pub and bought a bottle of champagne. Silly, I know, but it was the first bit of good news we'd had since this nightmare started and I wanted to mark it. We drank to Ben and hoped that wherever he was he had heard and was happy. Friends who'd heard the good news on television started to turn up and again we sat round, as if at a campfire, and told our favourite stories about him, each trying to tell the craziest and funniest, of which there were many.

One girl who was a friend of Ben's knocked on the door with a jumper of his – it turned out he'd worn it that night and must have left it in the pub when he got locked out. It hurt me that my poor brother had gone through all that without even a jumper on to keep him warm, but when I saw it was one of his very favourites, and realized it still smelled of him, I was only glad they hadn't ruined that also. We gave it to the girl to remember him by and continued telling our stories, eventually stopping not because we'd run out of tales to tell, but simply because we were all exhausted.

We woke up the next day to find that in the light of our public press conference, and the fact that the media had highlighted Ben's story so much, the nation had taken us to their hearts and had decided that enough was enough. They were shocked by Ben's death, and by every other child's life that had been lost in this dreadful way before him, and were determined to stand up and fight in my brother's name. When they picked on my brother that night, it turned out they had picked the wrong boy and nobody was going to let them – or anybody else – continue to get away with these murders if they could help it. We were so thankful that the nation seemed to be behind us but thought the interest would wear off quite quickly and everybody would soon go back to their own lives. Thankfully, we were very, very wrong.

Chapter 3

Do you remember the first time I was allowed to babysit you? I was about fifteen and you were five or six years old. Mummy and Daddy had to go shopping and I was trusted to look after you for an hour until they got back. I was so proud and felt so grown-up. Being the eldest, I often acted like your second mum anyway, but now I got to play it for real.

When they left, you were playing outside the house with your friends. I kept an eye on you out the window, a little skinny boy wearing only a grubby pair of shorts, even then the life and soul of the party. Other kids flocked around you – younger kids, older kids – you had this aura that just made everybody want to be your friend. I remember thinking babysitting was easy until the next time I checked on you, when I saw you huddled in the middle of your little crew, whispering furiously and laughing loudly. I wondered what mischief you were planning, I wondered if I should bother to stop it but decided that whatever it was, it couldn't be that bad. How wrong I was.

Why Ben?

Five minutes later the doorbell rang. I looked through the spyhole to see you standing there with a cheeky grin, surrounded by your little army. Thinking you just wanted to supply everybody with sweets or crisps as usual, I opened the door widely to be greeted with, 'Go! Get her! Throw 'em now!'

"Em' turned out to be a collection of insects that you'd run around collecting with the purpose of torturing me. You knew I was a typical girl who hated creepy-crawlies but thought it would be hilarious to torment me with my worst fear. Looking back it probably was – I remember me screaming, I remember you all laughing, I remember your laugh being louder and cheekier than any other. But at the time it wasn't funny, especially considering what happened after.

My first instinct was to slam the door on you, putting a barrier between me and those vile creatures. I did just that but after pushing hard for a few seconds, I realized the door was stuck on something and wasn't shutting properly. I continued pushing it with all my strength until I slowly became aware that above the screams of laughter and mania, there was a different type of screaming altogether. And it was coming from you. I wrenched open the door to find you standing there, tears streaming down your face and your little finger squirting out more blood than I had ever seen. One by one, the other kids fell quiet as I just stood there in horror, fighting not to pass out at the sight of all that blood. The thing that had been stuck in the door was your tiny little finger and in trying to force it shut I had ripped the top of it off. My first time babysitting and I had dismembered my little brother.

I started sobbing myself, saying 'sorry' over and over again as I rushed you into the toilet to try and stop the blood. At the sight of my tears, you stopped crying immediately and told me that it was OK and it didn't hurt that much anyway. Even then you were so very, very brave. I tried running your finger under the tap but it wasn't working and I started to get into a panic. It didn't help when one of your little friends brought the tip of your finger in for me to try and 'stick it back on'. Thank God Mummy and Daddy came in then and, being the real parents, calmly took control of the situation, rushing you to hospital so they could fix you. I sat there shaking and crying, wondering how much trouble I was in and if you'd ever forgive me.

When you all got back, I prepared myself for the worst but was instead given big cuddles by Mummy, Daddy and especially you. Your finger was fine – well it would be eventually, though you would always have a little scar. You had told Mummy it was all your fault anyway and told me that it really didn't matter that I hurt you and went straight back out to play and show off your battle wounds. I remember that day vividly, as did you, and years later you would still tease me about it and tell everybody about the time I chopped your 'whole' finger off.

There were many more times over the years where you hurt yourself and I worried, but none so much as that first time. You broke eleven bones in your life and hurt yourself countless times over, causing us all to panic, but you were always OK in the end. Eventually, the next time you broke something we would laugh as it was now expected and it didn't matter because you were always fine in the end. You were just the unluckiest boy ever but with the strength to get through anything. You were the cat with nine lives. We never, ever dreamed that one day those lives would run out.

For somebody who adores being a big sister, I didn't start out that way. For the first child it's always hard when somebody else comes along and steals all the attention and I found it extremely tough. When my sister Jade was born, I'd had my mum to myself for three years and didn't want to share her. Shortly after Jade was brought home, she was lying in her cot and I pretended to lean over and give her a kiss but instead poked her hard in the eye. I was extremely satisfied hearing her cry. I didn't want or need anybody else in my life and resented this little dumpling that had come along and taken over.

However, as time went on, she grew up and instead of being an annoying little sister, she became my best friend in the world and still is. We invented countless games together, we held hands wherever we went – even at night I would dangle my hand down from my top bunk bed and she would reach up from the bottom and we would fall asleep holding on to each other. Every photo of us when we are younger shows me with a tight arm around her neck, holding her close, trying to protect her, even when she's clearly trying to squirm away and make an escape.

Jade and I have the same father but unfortunately, when I was about six and Jade three, our parents split up. Suffice to say our real dad wasn't the best in the world and we were raised practically single-handedly by our mum, which is why we are so close to her.

My mum has always been my hero. She had me at the age of twenty-one and although I wasn't exactly planned and although she was so young herself, she put her all into being a good mum. I have so many memories of her making my life happy – planting tomato tops on the floor and pretending they were spiders to make me laugh, baking cakes, reading books – she treated me like a little adult and her best friend and would even let me help her with whatever job she was doing to provide for us – whether it was unpacking bikinis when she worked in a factory or helping her learn the routes when she tried to become a taxi driver. She worked so hard to give us the best in life, most of the time working shifts in a pub to earn money for us all to live. It was in this pub that, a little while later, she met my future stepdad, George, who also had two young kids of his own, Christopher and Holly. When Mum and George knew things were getting serious, they decided to introduce us kids and a day out was arranged.

When I first met this new family, again I wasn't happy. In fact, I refused to even get out of the taxi to meet them. I liked things the way they were – me, my mum and Jade – and I didn't want anybody else interfering, especially a stinky brother who was six months older than me. I liked being the oldest, I didn't want him taking over. However, like Jade, these new people won me round, especially

George. Over the years he went from being my stepdad to simply being my dad, although it wasn't an easy journey.

My dad will admit himself he is never one to show much affection and can be quite strict and grumpy, something Jade and I weren't used to, having lived with our smiley mum who gave us as many kisses and cuddles as we wanted. These differences made it hard for us to get on at first and we used every cliché in the book whilst growing up, including the age-old 'You're not my real dad, you can't tell me what to do!' We gave George quite a hard time and this lasted up until I was twenty-one, when I grew up and realized the sacrifices this man had made for me and the fact that he had taken us on and brought us up when our own father couldn't or wouldn't. Now I love my dad with all my heart, he has made me who I am today and even if I did think he was too strict at times, I can now see it was only ever in my best interests. The biggest thing I will always love him and thank him for, though, is that he gave us Ben and Georgia.

When Ben was born, there was none of the jealousy I had experienced with Jade. She had taught me that having younger siblings was the best thing in the world and being a little bit older and wiser, I couldn't wait for another one to play with. The night he was born, we were staying at my grandparents' house and were woken in the early hours of the morning by the phone call that told us we now had a little brother, Ben Michael Kinsella. My granddad knocked on all his neighbours' doors handing out cigars, while Jade and I ran up and down the street shouting, 'It's a boy! We've got a brother!' I remember to this day how happy I was.

The next day we went to school and when my dad picked us up at home time, all we could do was talk excitedly about the new baby and I asked what he looked like. 'Ugly thing,' replied my dad. 'He's got lots of hair and a big nose.' We were so disappointed when he told us that my mum and Ben weren't home yet but that we would go to the hospital to see them later. However, when we got in, there was my mum waiting to surprise us with a tiny beautiful bundle, already smiling that smile we would grow to love. He wasn't ugly at all, he was beautiful.

I'm the first to admit I was not a good-looking baby. I joke that I got all the brains, Jade and Georgia got the looks and Ben got the wit and charm. However, Ben was beautiful too. It wasn't fair. I keep going on about Ben's smile but unless he has turned it on you full beam, you really wouldn't know how warm it could make you feel. He had sticky-out ears that earned him the nickname 'FA Cup', but to make up for this he also had the longest eyelashes you'd ever seen. My mum gave birth to four children and decided to give the eyelashes to the only boy.

Growing up, Ben was a typical little boy. He would eat dead wasps out of curiosity, was obsessed with Thomas the Tank Engine and Noddy, and had a passion for football and Arsenal, courtesy of my dad. He was brilliant at art, something I think he got from my mum but which she denies. His handwriting was always terrible but his drawings were full of the most beautiful details. After he died, I was sorting through my things and found drawings he'd done for me as early as three years old. I was so happy that I'd kept them and they now have pride of place in my house, something he would kill me for, having produced a much better standard of work since.

He was the funniest little thing growing up. It was so strange having a boy around but I didn't know how we'd lived without him. He brought a light to the house which grew bigger and stronger the older he got.

It is hard to say when Ben stopped being my little brother. Of course he will always be my younger brother but one day he was this cute and sometimes irritating cheeky boy and the next he was towering over me, with a deeper voice and a maturity that shocked me. I'm not sure where he got his height from, as both my mum and dad are shrimps, but compared to the rest of us he was like a giant, and skinny as a toothpick with it. He hated his body and was always moaning that he wanted to grow some muscles, to the point where he went to Holland & Barrett and spent a week's pocket money on protein shakes he believed would turn him into Hulk Hogan. We told him not to be silly, and although we worried because he was so thin, we told him he had all the time in the world to get strong and grow muscles. It turns out he hadn't.

It's things like this that keep me awake at night. Did the knife hurt him more because he had no fat anywhere on his body to protect him? If we'd encouraged him to bulk up, would he still be alive today? Always 'what if'.

The one thing that didn't change in Ben, no matter how old he was, was his constant happiness. Ben was the happiest baby there ever was – people would comment on it all the time. He won bonny baby competitions, he made people giggle, and this trait continued with him throughout his whole life. As he got older, he turned his charm and happiness into a skill. He was so laid-back and loving. He couldn't hold a grudge against anyone, no matter how much you hurt him.

I remember the only time we ever really had an argument, and what a row it was. It was over the stupidest thing but he was at an age where he had started to stand up for himself and wouldn't allow me to tell him off and I was furious that he dared to talk back to me. Horrible things were said, we both cried and it seemed like the row would never be resolved. My mum tried to smooth things over but we were both too stubborn to back down. I stormed off to my room, determined not to talk to him again until he apologized. I didn't have to hold out very long as five minutes later he knocked on my door and, gritting his teeth, said 'sorry' and hugged me. I knew that he didn't really want to do it, that he still thought he was right but that he had to as he couldn't bear arguing. I was so grateful he had, though, as even those few minutes of not talking to my brother had hurt enough.

That was Ben. He'd do anything to keep the peace whether by backing down and apologizing or lightening the atmosphere until you couldn't help but laugh. If my mum tried to tell him off, he would simply bear-hug her and swing her around the room until she gave up. If my dad lectured him, he would listen, as we were all more scared of my dad, but every time he turned his back, he would pull a cheeky face at one of us until we were cracking up with laughter and begging my dad to leave him alone. Teachers could never punish him, although he rarely needed it, and his reports were filled with remarks like: 'Extremely bright. A hard worker but talks too much and can distract others with his jokes.'

Since his death, I have heard many stories from his friends of how Ben used this skill to defuse any fights or confrontations he came across. He was always the first to stand up for somebody in trouble, to the point where a few months before he died, he was threatened with a knife for trying to stop a fight between a group of boys. He came home that night pale and shaken, and said that he'd thought his life was over. He'd faced bullies when he was younger and had had minor confrontations but this was the first time he'd been seriously threatened and you could see how scared he was. We listened in shock and wondered what to do – we asked him to be more careful and not to put himself at risk but there was never a chance he would obey that order. My brother liked to help.

A few weeks later, when he was at work, he looked out of the window and saw a group of youths trying to steal a bike. He ran out and began shouting at them and eventually got it back. There was only one of him and loads of them but he stood his ground and they left. We were petrified that they would come back and wait outside his work one night to get revenge and there were even silly rumours that his death had had something to do with that, but of course it hadn't. He could have turned a blind eye like many people older and tougher than him would have, but he couldn't stop himself from helping out.

There were many, many times when Jade and I would discuss Ben and worry about him walking the streets. We always used to say that if it was going to happen to anyone, it would happen to Ben as he was so unlucky. In fact, a couple of nights before Ben died, a friend of hers asked Jade what her worst nightmare was. 'My brother dying,' she replied. A few days later her nightmare came true. We worried that because Ben had grown up with girls, if ever he got into a fight he wouldn't know what to do, but this didn't stop him standing up for himself and for that I am proud of my brother. If ever a boyfriend hurt or upset me, he would hug me and say he would 'sort them out'. I smiled inside and thought that it was simply false bravado on his part, but I know that if it ever came down to it, he would indeed have done it. He would have done anything for his family.

The picture I'm painting of Ben may seem too perfect

but it really is an accurate description. If anything, it's not colourful enough. He was just like any sixteen-year-old boy: he could drive you crazy to the point where you wanted to kill him yourself, but he would always, always make you love him again. The most honest way to describe him would simply be to say that he had a heart of gold. At the time Ben died, I was teaching drama to a group of children and it was only when one of them said to me, 'All you ever do is talk about your brother,' that I realized how true it was. I never tired of talking about him, and still don't. It amazes me that with only sixteen years of life on this earth, he achieved so much and it's only this that makes me wonder if this tragedy was indeed his fate. Did he achieve so much so quickly because he only had a short amount of time in which to do it? It's a small comfort, but not much when I'm missing his laugh or his voice or his hugs.

I didn't fully appreciate how proud I was to be Ben's sister until he died and I saw that he had done something that few sixteen-year old-boys could do – he had made an impact on the world and united a nation. It's easy to love Ben if he's your own, and even if you met him only once or briefly, but I couldn't believe how many people offered their love and support to him having never met him at all. In the first few days after he died, we were in our own little bubble, grieving – we knew he'd made the news but we thought he would be forgotten about the next day when something or someone more important came along.

We should have known that a boy like Ben could never be forgotten, even by strangers.

The day that we first went to the morgue to see Ben, I got a call from one of his friends. She was fifteen years old and was devastated and angry at having lost him. She wanted to do something to show her love for him and her hatred for the culture that had taken him from us. She decided to organize a local march that day where we lived in Islington, London, in honour of Ben and to mark his death. She started a small Facebook group and sent a few texts asking people to join her and I told her that when I'd finished seeing Ben, I would join up with her.

When I arrived at the start of the march there were close to four hundred people, with more joining every second – all there for my brother. They had turned up with only a few hours' notice, taking the day off work or school to be there. Almost everybody was in a white T-shirt to signal peace – some had Ben's face on it, some messages of love for him – everyone had their own tribute to give. There was a gigantic banner that simply said, 'Why Ben?' and everybody was waiting patiently, waiting to start walking towards making a change. Of course, people would argue that what could one march for one kid possibly do, but it turned out it was enough. It would do a great deal.

The girl who'd organized the march was astounded at the enormity it had taken on. She stood at the front in a white T-shirt that simply said: '18th?' signifying that she could be the next teenager stabbed on London streets that year, number eighteen. I joined her at the front and a policeman came up to me. He paid his respects and informed me that despite having learned of the march only an hour before, he had gathered enough troops to escort us on our way, had planned and blocked off a route that would lead us past Ben's school and the place he was attacked, and was stopping traffic for us along the way. He lectured me gently that I should have informed him the event was going to be this big and I don't think he believed me when I said I never in my wildest dreams imagined that it would. Turning around I saw a vast number of camera crews waiting to broadcast this to the country and I think it was at that point that I realized my brother was going to be someone special. He wouldn't be able to be the best graphic designer or tattooist as he'd planned, but he would definitely make his mark in some way.

We slowly began our walk along the streets that Ben had lived in all his life. People looked out of their windows, and left their houses and shops to join us. People read our banners and saluted us and my brother, bowing their heads in sympathy. As we marched, everyone began calling out for change, chanting, 'Stop knives! Save lives!' and singing songs for Ben. I walked at the front holding hands with my two sisters and the lead of our family dog, Teddy, who was really Ben's dog. I have since seen pictures of Teddy leading that march and I know my brother would be in hysterics at that. My mum and dad didn't feel strong enough to come to the march but were watching it at home, just as proud as we were.

Our route took us past London Mayor Boris Johnson's house, where we all stopped. Angry members of the crowd began calling for him to come out and face us, to tell us what he was doing to tackle this devastating problem, but he wasn't in. Somebody made an amazing speech asking for him to come and help his community and we all applauded him at the end. Unfortunately, when it made the news that night, it was edited as if we were actually applauding Boris Johnson, which was not the case at all.

We wandered past Ben's school, where he'd spent five years of his life and which he had left only the week before. I'd been there many times before to pick him up or see him in performances and kept expecting him to run out with his blazer on and his tie crooked.

We finished our march at the spot Ben had been attacked. Already there were hundreds and hundreds of flowers there paying tribute to my brother and although they were beautiful, I could only focus on the few faded spots of blood on the pavement that I knew were his. As we all stood there praying, lost in our thoughts, the policeman from earlier came up to me and said that all the media had requested I make some sort of speech or a statement to sum it up. I stood there frozen. I was in no fit state to speak in front of hundreds of people. I hadn't organized this march and didn't want to take any credit for it and, quite simply, I didn't know what to say. After much persuading, I decided to just thank everybody and tell them that the march was now over. The policeman helped me up on to a wall and as I stood up, every eye and camera turned to look at me. My legs were shaking and I was about to break into sobs. I opened my mouth just to say thank you but instead, my voice began speaking words I never meant to say. To this day, I still don't know exactly what I said, I would have to go through the tapes again to tell you that, but I do know that the voice that came out of me that day, and every day since, was not mine but my brother's.

I am not crazy. I'm not saying I was possessed by my brother's spirit or ghost, but I do know that up until that moment, I didn't have any energy to fight. I didn't want to make a difference because what was the point? My brother was already gone and no amount of change would bring him back. I simply wanted to lie down and cry for him forever. However, Ben had different plans and as I spoke, I grew more determined. I thanked everybody and the media for their love and support, but I also begged every kid there and across the country to lay down any knife they were or had ever thought of carrying. I begged that we didn't lose any more kids to this horrific act and prayed that another family wouldn't have to go through what mine had. My speech only lasted a few minutes but it was enough. Something had sparked inside me. Maybe it was simply that I needed to keep myself busy for the next few months, or give myself something to do so that I didn't feel so helpless, or maybe it was just as I said, that

Ben had plans. However, if I thought that one march and one speech was going to be the end of it, I was very wrong. That was only the start of a campaign that began with the actions of one young girl and the voice of one young boy, and grew so big that it succeeded in changing laws and lives.

Chapter 4

We stand outside the room – it looks so innocent and ordinary, like it was designed by grandparents with flowers here and pastel colours there. It seems silly to be afraid of a room but I am. You would never guess that in that normal room was a box and that inside that box was you. We are scared to step into the room because we know that once we step out it will be the last time we ever see you – alive or dead, it doesn't matter, this really is the last goodbye.

You've been lying here in the funeral home for the past few days while family and friends pass by to visit. We've visited you a few times separately but today we all come together, so that we can be a whole family one last time.

You lie still and quiet, with your face so pale, even though we know they've probably put make-up on you to make you look better. I know you would hate this. You're not a girl, you wouldn't want to wear make-up and your friends have had to see you like this. I hope you're not angry. We dressed you in your *most comfortable jeans, and a new Ralph Lauren shirt. Me and Mummy went to pick it out for you and it was almost like old times, like we were simply buying you a present but, of course, we'll never get to do that again. We got the brightest-coloured one we could find. I really hope you like it.*

We were going to buy you new shoes but a few days ago we had a message from a psychic friend who said that you didn't want any. We didn't know whether to believe this or not but instead we put you in the Prada shoes I bought you six months ago for Christmas. When you opened the box your whole face lit up and you hugged me so hard and told me I was the best sister ever. They were your 'going-out' shoes, your pride and joy and you wore them all the time. I didn't have the heart to tell you that I'd bought them on eBay and was pretty sure they were fake. They came in a terribly fake box and so I went back on eBay and bought a real Prada one and wrapped it all up nicely for you. I did plan on telling you but you loved them so much and I didn't think you'd ever notice. But now we have to bury you in them and I don't want to. You don't deserve fake shoes – if you are to spend eternity in them, you deserve real Pradas, but at the same time, I want you to have something from me, something that's been worn and loved by you, something you can take with you into your next life.

Your hair has been styled by somebody else and it's not the way you like it. We all try to do it in our own way but we still can't get it to look like it usually does, to look like Ben. They've cut off some of your hair and put it into an envelope for us to keep, and even though it's not attached to your body any more, even though it's effectively dead like you, it is still the most beautiful, bright colour. Months and even years later, the colour will still be there but you will not. It isn't fair.

We've brought some souvenirs for you, things for you to remember us by, because where you're going, you might meet lots of new, exciting people and we don't want you to forget us. We put in our favourite pictures of us as a family, we put a cross and chain around your neck and a mobile phone with some credit on in case you can call us. You never know. Daddy takes off his wedding ring and carefully puts it in your pocket so that if you fall in love with an angel up in heaven, you can ask her to marry you.

I want to give you more. You're going on an impossibly long journey and I want to make sure you're prepared but there isn't enough room in the box. I want to give you your Xbox and your football, and all the clothes you worked so hard to collect, but all the room is taken up by your little body.

We stay as long as we can but we finally have to go. When you know it's the last goodbye it's the hardest thing in the world to walk away. Please believe me, Ben, we don't want to. We don't want to leave you and I would climb in with you if I could but we have a big day coming tomorrow. We have your day. We kiss you for the last time and each have our own few minutes with you to say any final words. I can only say I love you. And that I'm so sorry I will never get to know the man you would have become. We walk out crying but we can't bring ourselves to end it all and say goodbye. Instead we *simply say goodnight as they close up the box and take you away for good.*

It seems strange and inappropriate to describe my brother's funeral as a celebration but I'm proud to say that's exactly what it was. What should have been the most tragic day of our lives – and don't get me wrong, it most certainly was – was also made slightly happier as we saw just how many people loved and were touched by our beautiful Ben.

We weren't able to bury Ben until almost three weeks after he'd died. The reason for this agonizing wait is that the 'other side' – the name by which we would come to call our enemies, the defence team – kept ordering more tests and more reports to be done on him. Because there were three men accused, each team wanted another chance to try and find evidence to prove it wasn't their client that had killed my brother. Not only did this mean we had to wait to put him at peace, it also meant they kept cutting and re-stitching his body again and again. It wasn't enough that he had died suffering and in pain, they still couldn't leave him alone. When we went to see him for the last time in the funeral home, we were told sensitively not to try and look at or hold his hands. We were so confused and upset, as this was what we wanted to do more than anything, but the undertakers couldn't give us any more information. We later found out that the reason Ben's hands were covered up was because, while performing all their tests and experiments to try and get their clients off, they'd had to peel the skin from my brother's hands to look for clues. This inhumane act seemed even worse than the eleven wounds we'd been told he'd received and I will never forgive them for this. We had held his hands throughout the sixteen years he was alive and now, when it mattered the most, we weren't able to.

While we were waiting for a date to say goodbye to Ben, our priest suggested that we hold a midnight memorial service for him. Instead of in a church, it was decided that we would hold the service at the spot where he'd been attacked, where there now stood hundreds upon hundreds of flowers in tribute to him. Although this spot held horrific memories, although it was the last place my brother had been fully conscious and alive, there was still something extremely peaceful about it. Me and my sisters would often go up and sit on the pavement there, usually at night, for in the day it was hard to find a moment where there weren't other people there mourning him. We'd sit and light candles for him, and read all the beautiful messages that had been left for him – some sad, some hilarious – the best being the various pairs of knickers that girls had left with cheeky messages scrawled across them. We knew he'd have loved those. There were so many pictures of him that as a family we never got to see – Ben at school, Ben playing with his friends – and although we knew almost everything about Ben, we got to see other sides to him too. We got to see just how many friends he had and how much he was adored. Almost the entire pavement of York Way had been turned into a beautiful memorial wall for Ben and although soon it would have to be cleared away, for now it was a place where people could go and feel closer to him. Therefore, we decided that this was where we'd hold a tribute for Ben.

Once again, it wasn't my family who organized this – we simply didn't have the strength – but somebody kindly did and word began to spread. On that day, everybody I spoke to was sad and upset, sitting around waiting for that evening when we would all march up and pray for Ben. In contrast to our mood, the weather was beautiful. It had been a strange summer, but it was as if Ben was shining down, making his day extra special. I decided it was no good moping around waiting for something to happen. I decided that I was going to do something fun in my brother's name, something that had he been here, he would have appreciated.

I sent a message round to all his friends and mine and told them that I was going to hold a game of rounders for Ben. I went out and bought a rounders set, made up a little picnic and went over to the local park with my sisters to wait. Within an hour we had almost fifty people there – once again, word had spread. All of his best friends, people who were simply acquaintances, all of my younger sister's friends – they all turned up to play for Ben. People brought food and drink and music and soon a competitive game was under way. For the first time since my brother died, I laughed properly. I felt guilty as I did but it was so nice to see everybody having fun, to see people smiling again. Even my sisters were smiling. The game went on and on, nobody wanting to stop. At one point, a policeman strolled over and I thought they were going to shut us down for being too loud and rowdy, but he simply smiled and said he was just there to make sure we were all OK.

As the sun began to set, I called my mum and dad, and told them to come over and see what was happening. They were reluctant at first, they didn't want to leave the comfort of their house, they didn't want to laugh and play, but finally I convinced them. When they arrived, they couldn't help laughing too and amid cries and cheers of 'Come on, Deb' and 'Hit a home run for Ben', my mum even managed to pick up the bat and take a shot for her son. Watching her giggle as she tried to get around the course brought tears to my eyes and I hoped my brother was watching this spectacle.

Finally, it was time to pack up and get ready for that night. The fun and the laughter stopped and everybody made their way home, remembering why we'd been playing such a game in the first place.

At half past eleven that evening, I got in the car and made my way up to Ben's spot. As I drove, I witnessed an amazing sight. Loads of groups of people were slowly making their way there too, all walking, most wearing T-shirts and various items in honour of Ben. There were so many people and when I finally reached the service, I saw the full extent of it. Again, hundreds of people had turned up for him – of all ages and backgrounds – and nearly everyone was holding a lit candle in the air for him. It was almost silent and as I stumbled to the front, I was held up by many of my friends. I lit my own candle and then our priest began to conduct the service. There was a light-hearted moment when somebody's phone rang, interrupting him, but apart from that it was lovely.

At the end, there was none of the laughter that had been present at the end of the previous march for him, or indeed at the game that day – everybody was in tears and it seemed to be all too real now. I think people had been caught up in the hype and shock of what had happened. I don't think many, including myself, had realized that Ben actually wasn't coming back, but it seemed it was finally starting to sink in. That service was just an introduction to the real thing and a taster of the pain we would have to endure.

We finally got the date we were allowed to bury Ben – the eighteenth of July, the day before my birthday. In the past two weeks, it had been both my mum and dad's birthday as well, and every time one of us received a card that didn't have Ben's name in it for the first time, didn't have a jokey message followed by the words 'Love Ben', it was another blow to the heart. We hadn't celebrated my parents' birthdays and I definitely wasn't going to celebrate mine. In fact, with the anniversary of Ben's funeral running into my birthday, I didn't think I could ever have another birthday celebration again. Another thing ruined.

Planning a funeral is awful. There's so much to get through but every task is the last thing in the world you want to do. Nobody wants to pick out a coffin, or an outfit or music for somebody who has died, especially a sixteen-year-old boy. I'm a natural organizer and a great planner, and usually relish the chance to show off my skills, but this task seemed too big even for me. I wished that somebody else could have done everything for us but nobody knew Ben like we did and we wanted it to be perfect for him. Together, my family tried to make it as much of a tribute to Ben and his life as it could possibly be.

We started with the coffin, the new home that his precious body would go in. We didn't care about different types of wood and silks, we just wanted the best. We also wanted it to be as cheerful as Ben had been. My mum asked a friend who was good at art to help out and Ben's coffin was transformed. We painted it in his favourite colours, purple and yellow, and put Ben's emblem on the top and sides.

Ben was forever drawing and graffiti-ing and while growing up he'd designed an emblem of a 'K' surrounded by a crown that stood for his surname, and also his nickname, 'Kings'. He scribbled this everywhere – on books, on clothes, on walls in our house. Thanks to the media, since his death Ben's emblem had become recognized across the country. The *Sun* newspaper designed beautiful badges with Ben's 'K' on them and thousands upon thousands of people wrote in to get one. Everywhere you went, people were wearing Ben's badge and I know he would have been so proud that he had at least left a mark as a designer. Therefore, it seemed only fitting to paint this design on his coffin.

We debated whether to keep the church service a small, intimate event but we knew it wouldn't be fair to all those people who had known and loved Ben. Finally, we chose the biggest church we could, St John's in Duncan Terrace, Islington. This held one thousand people and although we never dreamed there would be that many people there, we thought it better to be safe than sorry. When the day came, to our surprise, even more people turned up. Those who couldn't fit into the church lined the streets outside, just wanting to be there to show their support. For a sixteen-year-old boy to draw such a crowd was amazing. I hope he was able to see how popular he was.

There were many little things to arrange for the day that kept my family busy – hymns to pick, food to make, memorial cards to design. However, none of us had the energy or, more importantly, the money to do all these things. I'll never forget the day my brother died, when we were all in the pub drinking away our pain, and I went over to my mum to find her crying. Thinking it was the fact she had lost her only son that day that was making her upset, I gave her a cuddle and tried to utter words of comfort that didn't help one bit. She turned to me and with pain in her eyes said, 'I don't even have enough money to bury my son.' It broke my heart.

Funerals, like weddings, cost money. If you're old and have planned for a funeral for some time, you may be OK, but if somebody rips your child from this world one day, and you're a normal, working-class family, you don't have money saved up for something like this. My mum would have been saving to buy Ben his first driving lessons, not his coffin. The worry over the cost hit me as well. We wanted the best for Ben – if he had to be buried we wanted to do it properly and, on top of all they were going through, I didn't want my parents to have a debt for their son's funeral hanging over them for years.

It is here that I must thank all our friends, our local community and everybody who helped take this worry from our heads for, without them, I don't know what we would have done. Nearly everything we needed was donated. The memorial cards, the food, the flowers – everybody chipped in and helped out and it showed that although something horrific had happened in our community, not everybody was bad and people still knew how to pull together in times of sadness. I know that we are much luckier than some families who have had to bury their loved ones and I can only say that we really are grateful to have such good friends. You all know who you are.

While people were helping my family organize the little things, I concentrated on making Ben's goodbye special. I didn't want a normal service – he was sixteen and hated going to church. Jade and I had attended Catholic schools all our lives and so were made to go to church on special occasions, though we too dreaded it. Ben and Georgia got off lightly and went to a non-Catholic secondary school and so they hardly went at all. I knew the church part of the service was important, for how else would he get to enter heaven, but I wanted to make it better for him in any way I could. If it were up to me, I would have had live bands playing and Lucy Pinder performing the service, but I didn't think that would be allowed.

At the time, one of my best friends, Sarah French, was playing the lead in the theatre production of *We Will Rock You*. I'd been to see her many times and she was absolutely amazing. One of my favourite songs from the show was 'No One But You (Only the good die young)' and when I first heard it, I announced that I wanted it played at my funeral, no matter how old or young I was. I never imagined that I would have to bury my younger brother in the next year, so I decided to loan him my favourite song for the day and asked my friend to perform it in the church. She agreed and that was one thing off my list.

Next, I wanted to make sure people remembered Ben exactly how he was. For those who hadn't been lucky enough to meet him, or who didn't really know the kind of boy he was, I wanted to make sure they understood. One of his friends had put together a beautiful video of him in the days following his death – a montage of pictures – funny ones, family ones, ones even I had never seen, and had also included moving images from the march and tributes that were held in his honour. I asked him if I could use it for the service and then went about finding the biggest television I could. Again, with the help of friends, a PA system was donated that took up almost one whole side of the church. When it arrived the night before and I went to help set it up, I was horrified. Surely, the priest wouldn't let me put this atrocity in a house of God? However, he gave permission and did so happily. He laughed and said that he'd never seen anything like it before but that it was Ben's day and he should have what he deserved. We gave it a test run and it worked beautifully, another thing ticked off.

The final touch was the music to be played. Ben absolutely loved music. He was always on LimeWire, downloading the newest tunes, while my mum fretted about it being illegal and lectured him that the police would come bursting in to arrest us all. He would simply laugh at her worry, slip his headphones on and get lost in his favourite music. We wanted the songs played to reflect Ben, we wanted to get it absolutely perfect. There were so many songs that he loved and of course we had no way of asking him now which ones he would choose, but I hope we did him proud.

With all the planning, there wasn't much time to think about the day itself and it came all too quickly. The day before, I realized that I didn't even have an outfit. Not that I cared about things like that at the time, but I did want to look my best for my brother. We had asked everybody who was attending not to wear black but to wear the brightest colours they could find. We also asked people to spread the word and come in funny sunglasses and wigs if they could, for Ben was obsessed with sunglasses and had many pairs in crazy colours and designs. There are so many photos of him with his sunglasses on and we thought it would be a lovely touch to the day. A few days before, my sister Jade had picked out a beautiful dress from French Connection and had paid an extortionate £120 for it. I had seen the same dress in a bright shade of yellow and wanted it myself but didn't want to pay so much money for a dress I knew I would never wear again, having worn it to my brother's funeral.

The day before the funeral, I went down to Camden to find a cheap and cheerful outfit and, of course, get my sunglasses to match. I wandered through the stalls and markets of Camden and got completely lost, as I tend to do. I turned a corner and bumped into my youngest sister Georgia, with a group of friends, who had also come to get her outfit. This was strange in itself as I had no idea Georgia was going to be there; in fact she'd said she was going to the West End, and to bump into her in the hustle and bustle of Camden was weird. We picked out our sunglasses together and even though I still had no idea what I was going to wear, I chose a bright-yellow pair simply because they stood out the most. I continued walking around the stalls, tired and upset now. I didn't want to be shopping, especially for this particular occasion. I wanted to go home, put my head on my pillow and cry. I found myself in a part of Camden I'd never been in before and was about to give up and get a taxi home when I finally spotted a dress. I walked over in astonishment, scarcely believing what I was seeing. There, on the only man-nequin outside the shop, was the bright-yellow dress that I had wanted. I turned the price tag over, expecting to see £120, and instead gasped in shock when I read '£20'. I ran straight into the shop like a whirlwind, startling the owner, and begged her to show me where those dresses were. 'I'm afraid that's the only one,' she said. It turned out that this tiny shop was a sample shop of French Connection that sold one-offs or faulty goods and that the yellow dress on the mannequin was the only one they had. With a heavy heart, I went back out to check the size, knowing that I couldn't be that lucky. But I was. I tried it on and the dress fitted perfectly, and when I handed over my twenty pounds I thanked my brother for saving me a hundred. I looked down at my matching yellow sunglasses and laughed for the first time that day. My sister wasn't laugh-ing, however, when I got home and told her the story. She was furious she'd paid so much money, and also said we'd look stupid if we both wore the same dress but I didn't care. My brother had given me this dress as a present and I was going to wear it proudly.

The day came and despite all the planning and the organizing, nothing could have helped us prepare for how hard it was. From the moment we woke up, we were all in tears and they didn't stop for a second. People and flowers began arriving early. I'd only been to one funeral in my life and that was my granddad's five years before. Most of what I knew about funerals was learned from films and books and it amazed me that there seemed to be only one way to get through it – to smoke and drink as much tea as possible. It makes me laugh the way we British deal with things and I sometimes wonder if tea and cigarettes should be diagnosed as a formal medicine, for even I found myself smoking and drinking lots – something I rarely do.

I looked outside the window and saw our square was covered in the most beautiful arrangements of flowers I'd ever seen. Big sunglasses, bottles of Magners, Ben's 'K' sign, an iPod, Arsenal emblems – there were even flowers from the Arsenal team themselves. You could see Ben everywhere, everything he loved was shown in the flowers and everyone that loved him was represented too. There were flowers from his primary school, his secondary school, his work, his football team – the messages were heartbreaking and beautiful. We had asked that people didn't spend money on flowers and instead donated to a charity we had set up in his name but that didn't stop the hundreds that turned up. There were still so many flowers that they covered the sixteen funeral cars that had been booked and then some.

Despite not wanting to spend a lot on flowers, as we

knew Ben wouldn't appreciate them – he was a young boy, what would he want flowers for? – my two sisters and I designed some special ones for him from the three of us.

Just weeks before Ben died, he got a tattoo. This was a big problem in our house. He had begged and begged my parents for months to be allowed to get one but they refused to budge. They said he was too young, they hated tattoos, they cost too much – they gave him many reasons but it wasn't enough to put him off. When he got his first proper job and started earning his own money, he tried again, saying that it was his cash to spend how he wanted. This was true, but my mum still said no. I begged him too – I detested tattoos and thought they were tacky, imagining him with an Arsenal cannon or an England flag, as my brother was very patriotic. I even said I'd pay him a hundred pounds *not* to get one but he was adamant it was what he wanted.

Finally, after months of badgering, my mum said that if he did well on his GCSE exams, she would at least think about it. Well, he aced his mocks and was estimated A-stars and that was enough for him. He didn't wait to get the final results of his real exams, he went down to Camden on his first payday with a couple of friends and got his tattoo. He called my mum after and told her, and she hit the roof, ordering him home immediately. He tried to reassure her and said it was 'only little', but he knew he was in big trouble.

When he crept in, we were all there waiting for him, my

mum and dad with faces like thunder. He couldn't help laughing though. He was nervous and had the giggles and he knew his laughter would get him off the hook, which it did. As soon as he laughed, me and my sisters began laughing and eventually so did my mum, though she still wasn't happy.

'It's not funny,' she said, 'you're in serious trouble!'

'Show me,' I demanded. 'If it's anything Arsenal it's getting lasered straight off!' He lifted up his trouser leg and displayed his tattoo, waiting for our reaction. It definitely wasn't 'little'. Up his leg, ranging from small to big, were three nautical stars. We were confused.

'What do they stand for?' asked my mum.

'It's three stars for my three sisters,' he replied. 'Georgia is the baby one, then Jade and the biggest is Brooke.' We all melted on the spot. He was still told off, he was still in big trouble but his tattoo *was* beautiful and it was for his sisters. I knew that my brother loved me but sometimes I worried that I was just a bossy older sister, a pain in the bum. To know that he loved us enough to get the precious tattoo he so wanted for us made me so happy. Again, when I think of things like this, I just thank God that he got the chance to do some of the things he wanted before he died.

Despite hating tattoos, when Ben died my family wanted to get one each to remember him by. He would be absolutely furious after all the hassle we'd given him but eventually my dad got exactly the same as Ben on his leg,

I got the same but smaller on my wrist, Jade got one star for Ben on her belly and my mum had 'Ben' written on her finger. Georgia was too young, and she pesters us daily about being allowed one, but my mum and dad aren't *that* lenient. Stars are a big reminder of Ben to us now and we all collect them – whether in the form of jewellery, ornaments or clothes, they are another symbol of Ben – and so me and my sisters chose to get our flowers to Ben made in the shape of three stars, growing from little to big, so he could have his sisters with him. There wasn't enough room on the tiny white card that went with them to say all I wanted to so I simply wrote 'Benjamina,' – his childhood nickname – 'I love you. You were a beautiful star and now you will shine even brighter. I miss you so much. I love you even more. B x'

It seemed crazy writing a message that I knew he probably wouldn't ever read but if there was the slightest chance he could, I wanted him to know how much I loved him. I suppose that's why everybody writes cards and messages to loved ones when they die, and why they talk to them every day in their heads – just in case they're still out there.

When I next looked out of the window, Ben had arrived. His beautiful bright coffin was visible through the hearse window and people had fallen quiet. Our family priest was also there and Ben was lifted out of the car and blessed in silence, then put back in for his journey to the church. We took our place in the car behind him and followed in

_____

silence, tears streaming down our faces. The police had blocked off a route for us and as we drove down the streets, people were lined up, saluting Ben and making the sign of the cross. People came out of shops and houses, policemen lifted their hats, many were crying – it was amazing.

When we got to the church, there were hundreds of people both inside and out, as well as press taking pictures. They were very respectful but it still shocked me that Ben was having such an impact. There were so many faces I recognized and loads that I didn't. Many of my old *EastEnders* cast mates came to pay tribute too, which was lovely. Ben had been so proud when I got the part in *EastEnders* and I was lucky enough to be allowed to give him and Georgia a tour of the set, which they thought was fantastic. He'd met many of my cast mates and as some of them had become my closest friends over the years, he had practically grown up with them, becoming their friend too.

Richard Taylor, the father of poor, murdered Damilola, was there too as well as police, MPs and many other people. As our family walked into the church, our first song for Ben began to play. We had chosen 'Ben' by Michael Jackson and it set everybody off immediately. I know it's a song about a rat but the words are beautiful and very true about our own Ben. I know that he'd find our choice funny.

We took our seats on the front row and Ben was

_____

brought in. He was carried by his closest friends and family. Most of the service is a blur. I think I've tended to block out the very painful things from my mind but I was told later that it was beautiful. I'd had nightmares the night before of me jumping on the coffin and trying to open it one last time, but of course I didn't. Everything went perfectly. Sarah sang beautifully, the video was wonderful and made everybody cry, and my sister Jade read out a wonderful letter to Ben that my mum and dad had written. She was the only one strong enough to read it but, naturally, broke into tears while doing so. They decided to talk *to* Ben rather than about him as it was his day and it was him we were all saying goodbye to.

'Dear Nuts,' it began. This was another one of his nicknames, given more recently because, like most teenage boys, he always seemed to have his hands somewhere around the region of his private parts. It drove us all mad and we were forever shouting, 'Get your hands off your nuts!' The letter went on to say how proud we were of him and how every one of us would miss him so much, including our dog, Teddy. As always, it was hard to fit all that needed to be said in one letter but they tried their best.

We asked his friends and other family members to do readings and seeing his best friends up at the altar crying as they read broke my heart. It hurt that they would never get to make a speech at his wedding or at a happy occasion, that the only tribute they could give to him now was in death.

It was all over very quickly and at the end our family priest, who was leading the service, did something amazing. He asked people in the church to shout out qualities they knew Ben had. Everybody was shy at first as shouting in church is not the done thing but, eventually, his traits were called out. 'Good sense of humour', 'Caring', 'Kind' – the list went on and on. I was slightly hysterical by now and remember shouting out, 'He was tall!' as if that was his best quality.

He then asked that we would take the qualities Ben had had and try to use them ourselves to carry on his personality. He made some promises to Ben, looking up at the sky rather than down at his coffin, and promised that he would carry on Ben's legacy, that he would ask God to look after him, that he would ask God to look after us.

Finally, it was time to take Ben to the cemetery to be put to rest. As the coffin was lifted to be taken out of the church, we played our final song for him. After much deliberation, we'd chosen Calvin Harris's 'I Get All the Girls', as it was one of Ben's favourites, despite him never getting all the girls, apart from as best mates. The church erupted when it began to play – people were laughing and crying and dancing in the aisles. As Ben made his way towards the door of the church, somebody began clapping and it was like a Mexican wave. Thunderous applause broke out throughout the church, with people shouting, 'Go on, Ben!' as if he was scoring a goal at Wembley. The applause carried out the church and into the streets and by the time I got outside, it was still continuing, people clapping loud and clear for my brother.

The drive to the cemetery was horrendous – only lightened when we passed KFC and I saw some of my friends had stopped to buy food. Some people may have been annoyed at this cheeky behaviour but I was thankful for the laugh it gave me and knew my brother wouldn't have minded, for when he was hungry, nothing stopped him eating.

I don't want to spend much time reflecting on the burial, as it was the worst part of the day. Watching my brother being lowered into the ground will haunt me until the day I die. All I wanted to do was jump down there and stay with him, anything to stop him being in the cold and dark on his own. The priest said a few words and my family led the throwing of flowers into the ground. I kissed my bright-yellow sunglasses and threw them in instead – so that he would have a pair up there with him. At that point my mum completely broke down. She had done so well and had been so composed but this was too much for her. We didn't want to leave him there but there was nothing more we could do for him. We could only hope that we'd done him proud on his sending-off and that he was finally at peace somewhere lovely.

We made our way back to the wake, which was held at a local pub, and spent the day trying to hold it together. There was nothing left to do, nothing to plan or organize, and it was very easy to fall apart now. I spent the day talking to old friends and family, saying the same things over and over, drinking too much but not being able to stop. Finally people began drifting home and I began to get emotional. I was tired and upset and just wanted to sleep forever. My boyfriend Ray reminded me that in half an hour it would be my birthday but I didn't care. I was about to turn twenty-five and had just buried my brother – why would I want to celebrate? However, my friends weren't having any of it. They took me to a bar across the road from the wake, bought me a bottle of champagne and counted in my birthday. I'd rung my mum and told her I would come home, wanting her to say she needed me, not wanting to stay out any longer, but she told me to at least try and smile for my birthday, that it was what Ben would want, and so I did. When the clock struck midnight, I accepted everybody's hugs and kisses and birthday wishes but the one person I wanted to hear it from wasn't there and never would be again. It hit me hard then and I asked Ray to take me home to my family.

As we got into the cab, the driver asked us what was going on and why there were so many people outside the bar. Ray told him we had been at Ben's funeral but didn't tell him who we were. The cab driver then told us that he had driven Ben to the pub that night, that he had taken Ben to the place where he was later killed. I was in shock. I didn't know whether to believe him, as I knew my brother hadn't had a lot of money on him that night and he certainly wouldn't have wasted it on a cab – he would have walked a thousand miles if it meant he could save his cash for a Magners. But I couldn't help wanting to believe him. This man had possibly seen Ben after I had for the last time; he may have been able to tell me something I didn't know about him. I quizzed him the whole way home – who was he with, what was he doing, did he seem happy? The driver said he was with some friends and that he was a lovely boy, laughing and joking and asking for the music to be turned up. It was only a five-minute journey so he didn't have much information and, like I say, I didn't even know if it was true, but I liked to think of my brother being happy that night, at least for a short while.

I went home and climbed into Ben's bed, looking around at his belongings that were already starting to gather dust. It was over. Ben was completely gone; there was nothing else left for us to do. Well, this wasn't quite true. We had a great deal to do. We had more occasions to come that would be hard, a court trial to get through and Ben's legacy to pass on. We might not have the energy yet but, as Ben had shown so far, he still had a lot to give to the world. He might not have been here in person but we would have to make sure his spirit was never forgotten. Now that he'd finally been put to rest, it was time to start the campaign that would try to change our streets, to try to stop any other lives being lost, to make sure Ben's death had not been in vain.

Chapter 5

The pavement feels so very cold on my so very punctured back. Everything feels cold. Numbness persists. As I stare up at my killer-to-be he feels not the slightest measure of remorse at what he has just committed. Instead his dark smile sickens me in ways I couldn't imagine. He holds a phone to me and clicks the button. Flash, my misery is a mere picture used to broadcast the monstrosity society has become. I can only wonder whether I deserve to die here, now. Was it all for a reason?

Blood escapes my wounds. Blood once destined for greatness now seeps into the drains and the world beyond them. It all goes black.

'No, no, no, no, no – Please, God, no! This isn't real . . . this isn't happening! No, not to us. Baby, everything is OK. You're OK, you're fine, just stay with me, don't ever leave my side. Help is coming. Baby, open your eyes. I need you awake!' Sweet perfume grips and pulls me back into consciousness and as my eyes draw near, I see the bearer of my death has

been replaced by the bearer of my happiness – my partner, Molly.

Her screams torment me. I try to comfort her but my throat is filled with a thick mass of blood. Drip, drip. It continues to scurry around the pavement like the animal from the scene of this crime.

I hear new voices, see new faces. Fluorescent yellow prevails. My eyes meet darkness once more. I awaken to the smell of bad food reinforced with disinfectant. Yet this sweet, familiar perfume saves me for the last time. The angelic smell is drowned by the bitter moans and whimpers of the people around me.

I'm in a hospital. I've been stabbed. Three times in the chest, twice in the back. Once in the gut for good measure. Although I'm surrounded by family and friends, I'm the loneliest person in this world.

My pupils focus and I match the perfume to my lover. 'Oh, Molly, you don't deserve this. Will I marry you, Molly? Just reassure me you're mine forever and nothing else matters.' Tubes in my throat stop me from saying this to her. But I know she hears me.

I babble on. 'You tried to warn me he was dangerous. He was not to be messed with but I could not let him mess with my Molly. I never listened. I met my match. I paid the price. I'm sorry.'

And that's when it happened. It felt like I was a damaged battleship sinking into the sea never to return to the surface.

The world turned black. The smells, sounds, faces, feelings all disappeared. No white light, no flashbacks, just darkness.

Loneliness. I knew I was gone and couldn't ever come back. I just wished I had the strength to say goodbye. I was dead now.

The above is an extract taken from a story that was written by my brother a couple of months before he died. I found it a few days after his death while searching through our computer for every picture we had of him, every drawing he had ever done, anything to prove he had actually been here. It was titled 'Ben's Original Writing' and when I opened it up and began to read it, I was paralysed with shock. The details of his story were horrific and upsetting in any case, but the fact that they mirrored his own death only weeks later sickened me. He had even named the exact wounds he would later receive. It was extraordinary.

Had he predicted his own tragic death? Did he have some inkling when he wrote those words that he was narrating his own future? Had he jinxed himself by writing such dark thoughts? Or had he simply been an amazing English student who was given a task and had produced a story so heartbreaking, never knowing he wouldn't live to see the A-star he was awarded for it?

I was intrigued and needed to know why my brother had chosen to write about this. We asked his English teacher, who said that no specific subject had been set – the students were simply asked to write an original piece based on their own or a fictional character's pretend deaths. It sounded strange and morbid, however most students had taken the comedy route, producing funny and exaggerated stories – but not my brother. His teacher said how she had cried when she read it and knew that he had a special talent.

I couldn't believe that a boy his age could write so beautifully and produce a story that could strike fear and devastation in every adult and teenager. He had described what it was like to be stabbed, without even knowing what it felt like, without knowing he would shortly have to experience that pain. Surely his story would make people wake up and see what using a knife could do?

I decided I wanted the world to read the last story Ben had written. With my family's blessing, I asked the *Sun* newspaper if they would print it and thankfully they agreed. A few days after he died, Ben's last story was published. In just a few short days he'd become a designer and a writer – something he'd wanted all his life but could only get now it was over. When people read Ben's story, they began to see what I and my family had known all along – here was one special boy.

I know that every child is special. And even if they aren't, every child has somebody who thinks they're special. I know I must sound biased when I'm talking about my brother but I think it's something more than just having had the pleasure of being his biggest sister. I think if he hadn't had that special quality about him, the nation wouldn't have been as devastated as they were at his death and he wouldn't have had the impact that he did.

It's easy to say this happened simply because I was in *EastEnders* and was 'high-profile'. I even started off believing that myself. But the fact is, I hadn't been in *EastEnders* for almost four years. I could walk down the street and not be recognized for days, compared to a time when I couldn't get ten paces without being stopped for an autograph. I was in no way 'high-profile'. In business terms, I was probably closer to being 'washed-up' and so, although putting the title '*EastEnders* Star's Brother' in the headline made the story a little bit more newsworthy, I know that if it wasn't for the kind of boy Ben was, he would have been forgotten in a couple of days.

Of course, that doesn't mean that any other child who was killed through knife crime was simply forgotten. When the campaign for Ben started, I was wracked with guilt because I didn't want people thinking that I believed Ben was worth more than any other child. To my family he *was* the most precious thing in the world, but I knew that every child lost had somebody who loved them just as much, somebody who wanted recognition and justice for them also. At first I was scared to speak out because I didn't want to be hated. There were a few messages left on certain websites: 'Why is your brother any different from any other kid?'; 'He was probably flash because his sister was in *EastEnders*, he deserved to die.'

However, the good messages far, far outweighed the bad. People showed so much support, begging me to try and use the tragedy that had befallen my family to make some kind of difference for the world their own children would grow up in. They told me that I had a voice that would be heard and that I should use it to do some good. I realized that I didn't have to campaign just on behalf of Ben, I could fight on behalf of every kid that had been taken. Yes, it was Ben that drove me and put the words in my mouth, it was his death that had led me in this particular direction, but I could talk on behalf of every kid that had been stabbed to death both before and after – as sadly, it didn't stop with my brother. In the coming months, the list of children never coming home again grew longer and longer – Shakilus Townsend, CJ Hendricks, David Idowu, Joseph Lappin – and those that came before – Robert Knox, Jimmy Mizen, Martin Dinnegan – stories I had read and brushed aside, assuming it would never happen to me.

Every time I read a message of support I was so grateful but at the same time petrified. What did I really think I could do? What could one girl do that countless others before had not been able to? There that so many organizations that had worked their whole lives to try and make a difference, so many families that had been campaigning for years and had gotten nowhere – I didn't think it was fair that just because I used to have some sort of public profile, I could automatically get my voice heard. I knew that if the tables had been turned, I would have felt frustrated and angry that a twenty-five-year-old girl and her brother were getting all the limelight. Also, I wasn't even sure if I wanted to speak out. It felt too late. I hadn't spoken out when it had happened to sixteen other children in my city this year – if I had, maybe my brother would have been here today. There were thousands of people who'd never been affected by knife crime but had tried to make a difference and I hadn't been one of them, so wasn't it a bit hypocritical to jump on the bandwagon now?

These doubts drove me crazy and, coupled with the fact that I didn't have the energy or the motivation to fight, I thought about giving up before I'd even started. In all honesty, what was the point? Nothing I did would bring my brother back and, as that was all I really wanted, was there any point in getting involved? Selfish, I know, but I thought it was best I was completely honest with both myself and others. Was I just looking for a quick fix to keep myself busy or was I somehow deluded and thinking that if I fought hard enough, God would reward me by magically giving my brother back?

As always, it was Ben who pushed me into making my decision. I was sitting up in his room where we all spent most of our time, sniffing his clothes and trying to breathe in any scent that was left of him, while raiding his room for anything that would bring me closer to him. I would never have dreamed of doing this when he was alive – we weren't that kind of family and believed all of us were entitled to our privacy, Ben even more so because he was the only boy. I felt so guilty for snooping around and knew that he was probably looking down and telling me off. It didn't matter that he was gone and wouldn't be using any of this stuff again, these were still his belongings and I didn't really have a right.

I don't even know what I was looking for – a secret message he had left that said how much he loved us, a clue as to why this had happened to us, but of course I found nothing like that. His room was a typical teenage boy's room – but perhaps less embarrassing. There was nothing sinister or forbidden to find. The worst I came across was a solitary condom in a dusty packet that almost gave me a heart attack until I realized it was probably something he and all his friends had carried about in their pockets to seem cool, and not something he would have used anytime soon considering the dust. It struck me that I would never get to have those special conversations with my brother – not the 'Are you having sex yet?' because what big sister wanted to talk about that, but simple chats about girls and being in love and just giving him advice.

He had recently had his heart broken by his first proper girlfriend. Actually, he'd first had his heart broken by a girl at the age of two, when he'd fallen in love with a little mixed-race girl in his nursery. She wouldn't show him the slightest bit of interest and so one day he went into a corner and tried to paint one whole arm brown in an effort to look more like her, hoping she'd notice him then. She sadly didn't and for most of his life after that, he was always 'the funny best friend' rather than the boyfriend.

One day, he announced he had a girlfriend. He had fallen completely and utterly in love with her and brought her home and proudly introduced her to my mum, smiling widely and saying, 'Isn't she buff, Mum? Isn't she the most beautiful girl in the world?' The poor girl blushed bright red but that was how my brother was. If he loved someone he would let them know. For a few months we hardly saw him as he followed her around everywhere. She lived quite a way away and every night he would take her home on the train before making the long journey back again. We always worried about him travelling that distance on his own but he was a true gentleman and loved acting like one.

On their first and only Valentine's Day, he saved up and bought her an array of presents, the like of which I had never been given myself in all my life. He bought her favourite perfume, he gave her a tiny engagement-ring charm and made up a snow globe with a picture of them kissing. My eyes watered at the sight of him lovingly wrapping all his gifts for her and then turned into tears of laughter when he went around adding lots of jokey presents to wind her up. He made up a bag of random objects – an Action Man, a coconut, an old dog's bone – and presented it to her in all seriousness. She had a tantrum and then calmed down when she received her 'real' presents, but it annoyed me that she didn't share his wonderful sense of humour.

We always knew it wouldn't last – he clearly adored her

much more than she did him – and when she finally dumped him, he was devastated, though he tried hard not to show it. At the time I was furious that somebody had caused him pain, but now I would have given anything for that to be the worst and only pain he had to experience. I would rather his heart were broken a thousand times than stabbed just the once.

Continuing my search of his room, I came across his schoolbooks in the corner. I sat down to look through them and began crying when I saw work dated only weeks earlier. It was so strange that he had been here living and breathing just a while back, that our world had been normal until only a few weeks ago, for sometimes it felt like he had never been here at all. As I looked through his English book, I saw the first draft of his original writing story and cried harder. His writing was so messy and almost indecipherable but his words were powerful. Turning the page, I saw a letter addressed to 'Mr Brown' and curiously began to read.

It turns out that another task my brother had been set was to write a letter to the Prime Minister campaigning against a problem in society. My brother had chosen youth crime and the devastation it had started to cause. I read sentences like: 'Since 2001, the number of attacks on innocent civilians has risen from 31,368 to a shocking 171,723' and 'if we continue to sit back and watch as it goes on around us, the figures will inevitably grow and grow and grow'. These figures were obviously made up but I understood his point.

My brother's ideas to stop youth violence were 'longer sentences for violent offences', as he felt that 'these teens will continue to attack if they feel there won't be a consequence'. He said, 'If they know that abusing someone else will mean a minimum of seven years in prison, I seriously doubt they would take the risk . . .'

He spoke about organizing a peaceful march to protest at what was happening on our streets and even went so far as to write a safety plan ensuring people had enough water and protection to look after them. It was again uncannily similar to the march we had recently organised in his honour to protest against his death.

He pleaded with our Prime Minister and said, 'Mr Brown, we as a community and a nation have to work together to stop this happening. The reality is murder is becoming a part of everyday life in society. You pick up any newspaper and what is spread across the front page? Young kids dead, Dad in coma or pensioner fights for life.'

He stated that the police must be given more rights to enforce the law, must be given more stop-and-search powers as 'every day, gangs on the streets are laughing at the powerless police'.

He finished his letter with the statement: 'No, change is not going to be easy. But as the leader of our country, it is your job to make sure we live peaceful, safe lives. At the moment we are far from it. Change is evident, let's start now.'

His letter took my breath away and made me feel very,

very ashamed. I was twenty-five, had lived over eight years longer than him, yet had no idea things were this bad. Granted, I was no longer hanging around on the streets of London, but I had a younger brother and sister who were. I should have listened more, done more. Ben had obviously done his research and knew so many stories of kids who'd been murdered, gangs who'd caused terror and he was worried enough to write a letter to Gordon Brown to ask him to put a stop to it. It was then that I decided that this would be my brother's legacy and I would do everything in my power to make it happen. He had wanted our streets to be safer and maybe it was too late for him but he could still get his wish. No, it wouldn't bring him back, but it would mean he had achieved something amazing and if that was the best I could get, I would take it. I would make sure that Gordon Brown got the letter that had been written for him and that he would wake up and take notice. How many more kids must die before our government began to do something about it?

I knew it wasn't going to be an easy task and I knew I couldn't do it on my own. Our biggest help so far had been the nation and the media but would they continue with their support or would they move on to bigger, more interesting things? It soon turned out I had underestimated the public and how angry they were, and also the strength and commitment of the media.

Throughout my career I'd had a love/hate relationship with the media. When you're in the public eye, and especially in a show such as *EastEnders*, it is a given that you'll end up in the newspapers. However, I was honestly one of those people who hated seeing themselves in print.

I started acting at the age of seven. My mum had enrolled me in the local drama school, Anna Scher's, not because I'd expressed any interests in acting, or was a little diva who wanted to be famous, or even because I had any particular talent in singing or dancing. Actually, I had zero talent in both of those subjects. The truth was I was an extremely shy child so my mum sent me along in the hope it would give me more confidence and allow me to make some friends. Despite all her efforts, I hated going to drama school and didn't seem to make any friends at all. Thankfully, my mum wasn't one of those pushy parents and when she saw how unhappy I was, she said I could leave whenever I wanted. Before I got the chance, though, something strange happened. It turned out that I did seem to have some talent in the acting field after all and, at the age of seven, I got my first break in the BBC children's TV show *Mud*.

This break opened up a whole new world for me. I may have hated drama school but I loved drama itself. I loved playing a part, escaping from myself, being somebody completely different. Over the years, I was lucky enough to get quite a bit of work and juggled my acting around my schoolwork and various other jobs, ranging from working in a café to a doctor's surgery. I even managed to fit a year of university in until one day I was given the part of Kelly Taylor in *EastEnders*. I went along to the audition and got the call to say I'd won the part not even an hour later while I was on the bus coming home. To begin with, it was for eight episodes and I was over the moon, as was my family. Like most families in Britain, we had grown up watching this iconic show and they were all so proud of me.

My first days on set were petrifying. I was doing most of my scenes with Michelle Ryan, who played Zoe Slater, and Jessie Wallace, who played her mum, Kat. I'd watched these two ladies on my TV for the past couple of years and was so star-struck at meeting them. Unfortunately, my storyline was filmed away from the Square as Zoe had run away and ended up working as a prostitute, where my character was introduced. This meant I didn't get to see much of the famous set, or any of the other characters, but it was enough for me. I did my few weeks filming and enjoyed it, then walked away to go back to my life at university.

A few months after my storyline had been aired, I had a call from my agent. He'd spoken to the producers of *EastEnders*, who'd said that the public had liked my character so much, they wanted me to come back for a few more months. I was gobsmacked. I couldn't believe this was happening. I wanted to say yes immediately, but there was a lot to think about. It was OK doing a few episodes of *EastEnders* but I knew that if I went into the show as a more regular character, it would change my life forever.

I wouldn't be able to finish university, I wouldn't be

able to walk down the street as a 'normal' person, people would now be interested in me and my private life – and that meant it wasn't simply my decision. I had a family to consider too. I didn't want their lives to change because of me.

We all sat down and spoke about it and my parents said that, as always, it was my decision and they would support me in whatever I chose. My brother and sisters were so excited that I might potentially be famous and were only interested in what presents I could buy them. I finally decided it was too good an opportunity to turn down and entered the show as a regular in 2001. What started out as three months became six, and that turned into almost three years.

They were some of the best years of my life and also some of the hardest. I loved working on the show, I loved having a regular acting gig and I loved, and still do, the friends I made. However, as I feared, my life changed completely. I couldn't go anywhere, or do anything, without people trying to find out what I was up to.

I'm not one of those people who hate the paparazzi and I fully understand that if you sign up for this job, they come along for the ride. However, I was there from the age of eighteen to twenty-one and, like most girls that age, loved going out for a drink and a dance with my friends, only now I found there was always somebody waiting to catch me looking a bit the worse for wear. I didn't mind this so much, but I hated it when I was out with my brother or sisters and they would jump out on us, scaring the life out of them, or when they would post letters through my door, asking my mum to divulge her deepest, darkest secrets. You can mess with me all you want, but nobody upsets my family. Over the years I got some bad press, such as silly kiss-and-tells, and bad reviews, but also lots of good. I met lovely reporters and photographers and learned that not all the media were bad, though I would still choose to keep my distance.

Now, however, I needed their help more than ever. At first I had hated that they were constantly knocking on the door asking us for interviews about Ben's death – we were having a hard enough time as it was – but I knew that if I wanted to get my campaign going, and if I wanted to reach Gordon Brown and the important people, I would need the media completely on my side.

Thankfully, they all were from day one. It's very rare to get any newspapers to work together and also to get any newspaper to support you for any length of time, but since the day I started campaigning against knife crime, nearly every paper has been amazing. The *Sun* and the *Daily Mirror* rarely work together or do interviews on the same subject but, for once, they laid aside their egos and each helped me in their own ways – the *Sun* most importantly by designing Ben's badge and the *Mirror* by starting their anti-knife campaign and using my brother's face and the slogan 'For Ben . . . for everyone'. They still use this to this day and although again I worry about him seeming more important than anyone else, it is still lovely to see his little face associated with such an important cause. It was going to be a long, long journey to get to the right people and would take lots of hard work to achieve any goals at all – especially as I wasn't even sure what they were yet. However, now that I had some powerful allies, I could at least make a start.

Chapter 6

Your exam results came today. We received a phone call from your headmaster, who said he was going to drop them in personally, as obviously you couldn't go into school and collect them yourself, couldn't go in and open them up and jump around in joy or despair with the rest of your friends.

When your head arrived, he handed over an envelope and, smiling sadly, said, 'He got some of the best results in the entire school. You should be very proud.' It was only me and Jade in the house and we were under strict instructions not to open them until the rest of the family got home. We sat there in silence, both itching to open that envelope. We always knew you'd get good grades but we wanted to see the proof.

I can't believe that you're not here to see the results of all your hard work. You were promised £100 for every A-star you got and I know you would have jumped up that morning, impatient to collect your prize. I can picture your little face smiling with excitement, but trying to play it down and act cool.

———

Mummy comes in and we hand her the envelope. She opens it and starts to cry – for a split second I think maybe you've got all Fs, but then I realize she's crying because you have done her proud. Indeed, when I look at the slips of paper I see that you got A-stars in Art and English, of course, and As and Bs in every other subject. I see your name, I see your date of birth and for once I can't see your date of death – it's as if you're still here with us and, at the very least, it's proof you were once here at all.

We smile proudly and I state that you still haven't beaten me, I'm still the winner when it comes to getting the best grades. I wish you were here so I could tease you about this. I wish you were here so we could all hug you and make a fuss of you, and you could enjoy the rewards of five years' hard work.

Throughout the day your friends knock on the door, all clutching their results. Some have waited until they got to us to open them and they do so, sighing with relief or crying that their parents are 'gonna kill' them. None of them has done as well as you and I know that you'd be there, trying to cheer them up, taking the mickey and pretending to show off when actually it was you that got them this far in the first place. They all say, 'He made me sit down and do my work, he told me to buck my ideas up . . .' You were a natural-born helper and I wonder who you've found to help now. I hope you'll still help us, as we certainly need it, especially on days like today.

We decide to go out and have a pizza for you – one of your favourite foods – and slowly people hear and begin to join us. There is a crowd and after a while I make a short speech and say well done to all the kids who got their results today. I name them all and they smile shyly, and at the end I say your name, for you're not to be left out. I feel silly and a bit embarrassed but just because you're not here, we can't take away what you've achieved. No, you will never get the chance to use these amazing grades but that doesn't mean we should just throw them away.

I imagine a different scenario – you standing next to me with a slice of pizza, smiling widely and saying, 'Come on, then, hand it over.' I imagine having to chip in towards the £200 for your fantastic grades and cursing you as I do so, while being the proudest sister ever at the same time. I imagine you spending it all at once, buying lots of nice new clothes for when you go off to college in a couple of months. I imagine your first day at col-lege, being all shy and scared again but covering it up, not wanting to worry us. I imagine you making friends, doing well, becoming a big boy and then a man, before becoming the best graphic designer or tattooist there ever was.

This is what should have happened, but this scenario was wiped out in a single moment of madness. All that talent, all that potential simply erased and all we have left to show for it is a piece of paper with your name on and a few pretty letters. If only they had taken one second to get to know you, had stopped to find out that you were a good boy, a clever boy, one who didn't deserve to be taken, maybe things would have been different. I doubt it, but maybe, just maybe, they would have let you live.

A couple of months after my brother died, we still had no reason as to why it had happened. Yes, there had been a fight earlier that night that he wasn't involved in, but may have been blamed for, and no, we probably wouldn't find out what had really happened until the trial – and maybe not even then – but what we couldn't understand was how it had been *allowed* to happen. Ben was already the seventeenth teenager killed in 2008, so why had nobody solved this problem yet? Why were children still being brutally murdered by other children?

In the weeks after Ben's death, I was asked to go on numerous talk shows and do interviews to give my opinions and solutions to the problem, but I soon realized that I didn't have any yet. I didn't know why my brother had been killed. I knew it wasn't down to gang involvement, or a drug war or even a racial attack, which were some of the reasons being given for knife crime these days – there didn't seem to be a reason. When I looked back at other cases, I saw that this was true of quite a few of them. Yes, there were cases where it had been gang rivalry or a stupid argument over a girl or a debt, but in many there didn't seem to be any explanation whatsoever. It was simply a case of angry, frustrated men thinking they could do what they wanted on the streets without any thought to the results or consequences. In my opinion, people didn't value life any more and were happily taking other people's and believing they could get away with it.

Although I was angry at the people who'd taken my brother, I was also angry at the systems that had stood back and allowed this to happen. Where were the police, the parents, the courts, the government when all these stabbings were going on? Had they taken appropriate action when the first boy was stabbed to death, maybe we wouldn't have lost so many more since.

However, I knew I couldn't judge people without good reason or just because I was so furious. I decided that to form a better opinion and find the best solution to this nightmare, I needed to go on a personal journey and figure out exactly what was going on in our country and who was really to blame. Was it bad parenting? Was it bad schooling? Was there not enough discipline and sentencing from the courts? I would find out one way or another who else was responsible for my brother's death, as it was the only way I would ever make sense of what had happened and be able to move on.

In the beginning when I gave interviews, I was asked, 'How do you feel towards the accused? Could you ever forgive them?' and worst of all, 'Why do you think they did it?' I hated those questions, mainly because I didn't feel I could give a truthful answer. It was too early even to be thinking about forgiveness anyway, and who could honestly ever forgive an evil act like this? And how did I feel towards them? Well, although I didn't want to waste any thoughts or energy on them at the moment, deep down I *hated* them. Not only for what they had done to my brother, but for what they had done to me and the family that had been left behind. They had killed us all. Never again would we get a good night's sleep without picturing my brother's body covered in blood, never again would we laugh or have a completely happy day. We couldn't function, we couldn't work, we simply couldn't live a normal life and they were the ones who had done this to us, so how did I feel? I thought they were scum. I thought they were evil, despicable people who didn't deserve to live when my little brother couldn't. But I felt I couldn't say this.

Our country seemed to have become extremely liberal and while I was all for this, while I didn't want us to be a cold-hearted and uncaring nation, I felt we had become too soft. Yes, there were people who'd had hard lives, had been born into poverty or abuse or crime and didn't have the same chances as others, but did this mean they had an automatic excuse to hurt people?

Some may think it's easy to say that in my position, that being in *EastEnders* and having the job I did meant I must have a good life and I could have anything I wanted. This isn't true. Yes, the money was better than working in McDonald's but that hadn't always been the case for me.

I had grown up with all the love in the world but not a great deal of money. My parents had six children between them to support, and support us they did, working as hard as they could to make sure we had what we needed – not what we wanted, but what we needed. Compared to my friends, I didn't have much at all and I have early memories of coming down in the middle of the night and seeing my mum sobbing at the kitchen table, her little book of debts in her hand, desperately trying to make ends meet.

We may have had more compared to others, but we could also have taken the view that we didn't have enough – we could've gone out and shoplifted or mugged people and blamed it on our circumstances but we didn't. Even after I left *EastEnders*, and work had dried up a bit for me, I went and worked in a butcher's for a few months, determined to pay my way, determined not to give up and take an easy route. This is how I was brought up – which leads me to the next excuse I was hearing: that there are some people in this world who've never been shown an ounce of love, support or discipline in their lives, and are therefore not capable of caring about anyone else. That some people have been so horrifically abused that they can't stop themselves from hurting others.

This I can sympathize more with. This I understand better than 'I want something so I'll take it and damn the consequences'. However, there are hundreds and hundreds of people who have lived this kind of life – I've read many of their stories and cried my eyes out at what they've been through but, despite this, most of them have turned their lives around and, in spite of all the hurt and pain, have gone on to produce beautiful, loving families themselves. They say they wouldn't want anyone to go through what they had to, but believe they've become better people because of what they have endured. It's stories like these that stop me believing that anyone who murders or hurts someone must obviously have had that bad a life because, again, it's not a good enough excuse. Everyone has the ability to make a choice in their life, everyone knows deep down what is right and what is wrong and, when it comes down to it, murdering somebody because you have had a tough time is not right.

What annoyed me the most, however, was that this didn't seem to be the problem in the majority of instances. When most teen-on-teen cases of violence came to trial, we weren't hearing that the accused had had such a horrific life, that he or she was mentally scarred and incapable of any other actions than those they had committed. What we were hearing was that there seemed to be a generation of fourteen- to twenty-five-year-olds who had no respect or regard for life. They would stab someone for a pair of trainers or a mobile phone, they would kill for a postcode (ironically, probably in an area that they moaned about and detested), and they would laugh while they were doing it because they knew that most of the time they would get away with it. As my brother had written, kids were laughing at the 'powerless' police and while they had no fear of authority, things would only get worse.

At the start of my journey, it seemed to me that people fell into two camps with different opinions on how to deal with this problem – there were those that demanded stricter jail sentences, tougher laws and more action, and those that said we simply needed to rehabilitate people and offer them a better life.

Why Ben?

I understood the second opinion, although I was very much in favour of the first. I could accept that if a young boy was sent to prison at the age of fifteen for dealing minor drugs, this would probably in the long run do him more harm than good. He would make better contacts in prison, learn more criminal skills and come out with a record that would stop him getting a proper education or a job. Then he would have no choice but to resort to crime and use his new-found skills to climb the criminal ladder, resulting in more serious crimes and, maybe even one day, murder. I could see this point and agreed with it. Maybe it was better to rehabilitate non-violent or minor offenders rather than just chucking them straight into prison. But when it came to those that had offended seriously, I believed it was a different story altogether.

Individuals who cold-heartedly murder another human being for no apparent reason are unlikely to be easily reha- bilitated – and if I'm completely honest, I don't think they deserve to be. I'm not talking about cases where the killing was an accident or carried out in self-defence, for which people should still take responsibility, I am referring to the minority for whom carrying a dangerous weapon around is a fashion statement – a mark of what a 'big' man they are. I'm referring to those who would use that weapon to harm another person without expecting punishment. They have knowingly made a premeditated choice. They know carrying a weapon is wrong. They can blame it on needing protection or having to fit in but, deep down, they are fully aware that the second they put that weapon in their pocket, there is a chance they could kill somebody or themselves. To anyone's thinking, surely they deserve the harshest penalty?

The liberal philosophy is that maybe these thugs have been brutalized themselves, and that they should be shown leniency and understanding, but at what cost to the victims' justice, or their families, or our society? What about the message it sends to our kids, who will start to believe that it's fine to commit such an act and not be seriously punished for it? When a dog savages somebody, it is immediately put down, and while I don't advocate the death penalty and am not naive enough to think we can simply apply the same practice to humans, I do believe we should definitely be looking at a form of punishment that acts as a deterrent – where the severest sentences await those who commit brutal murder. People shouldn't be sentenced to death, not only because if we look back through history, too many innocent people have been wrongly convicted and executed, but also because part of me feels it's an easy route out. Far better that they should have to sit and think about what they've done for years to come, and if it does haunt them and does make them become better citizens, then all well and good. However, I still feel it's unfair that they get to carry on with their lives when their victims can't.

In the US, a life sentence means pretty much that – thirty or forty years out of a person's existence. Time to reflect and pay their debt to society – not to the victims or their families, as nothing can bring back a murdered loved one, but at least I may be able to accept they've been punished appropriately. However, in England, life usually means between eight and twelve years and this horrifies me. If they're found guilty at all, the people who killed my brother will be out by the time they are thirty. They'll have enough time to start living again, to meet a nice woman, to have a family and maybe have some kind of a career and, in all probability, will have at least forty or fifty years left to enjoy on earth.

What kind of punishment is this?

My brother was in a box in the ground for all eternity and the most his killers would get was restricted freedom for probably twelve years. And that was only if they were convicted in the first place.

More and more criminals are being let off with a slap on the wrist or a caution for serious crimes simply because our prisons are too overcrowded. If the courts had given an appropriate jail sentence to anyone found carrying a knife the first time round, it might have shocked most of them and encouraged them to put down their weapons for good. It might have stopped them taking that knife out and using it the next time round. It might have saved somebody's life.

I couldn't believe that the government and courts were giving the excuse of overcrowded prisons as a reason not to send people to jail. One man who'd carried a knife on numerous occasions and then waved two knives in a man's face, thankfully not harming him but scaring the life out of him, was let off for this reason. If we couldn't afford to build prisons to solve the problem, then how could we afford to build a multi-million pound Millennium Dome that sat unused for years? How can we afford to spend billions on the Olympics?

As Ben also said in his letter to Gordon Brown, in a few years Britain is going to be the proud host of the Olympics, yet who will want to visit our country to see their heroes compete when there is the fear of being shot, stabbed and killed? Even at his young age, Ben could see the logic of spending money to make your country safe rather than spending it to show off. I reckon that if the government had bothered to do a survey and see where the real people wanted their hard-earned tax money spent, almost all of them would have chosen safety over a stadium.

These were my real and honest opinions, but in the beginning I felt I couldn't say them. For a start, I thought people would see me as an air-head 'celebrity' who didn't really know what she was talking about, and then I thought that if I dared to speak out about harsher punishments, there would be a backlash and I would lose any support I had. I wanted people to like me and I wanted people to believe in me and so I started off my campaign by saying that yes, we needed to understand the 'bad' children, we needed to identify them early on, help them choose the right path and provide them with better opportunities. But the whole time I was saying this I felt like a traitor – to my brother, to my family and to myself.

I really did believe in what I was saying. I did think that it was important to catch any kids that were going astray early and help them with their problems so they didn't become someone else's. I had taught 'problem' children before and rather than being disgusted when they screamed abuse or lashed out, I was heartbroken at the circumstances that had made them that way and wanted to erase the bad conditioning and let them start again. I did think that spending more time and effort on these kids would help, but I knew it wouldn't completely solve the problem.

More to the point, I was fed up of concentrating on the bad kids and wanted to focus on the good. It wasn't fair that all teenagers were getting this awful reputation due to the actions of the minority. I had a teenage sister and had, until recently, had a teenage brother and they were good kids. I found that the majority of messages and support I was getting were coming from the age group that everybody was talking about and condemning, and that they were strong in their opinions. They all said the same thing: this had to stop. Kids had to be deterred from carrying weapons, as they were all scared for their lives now and many believed that tougher laws were the only way to do this.

As I started speaking to more and more people, it became clear that this was the overall opinion everywhere.

People were crying out to be protected, for action to be taken. When something goes wrong, we automatically look to the police and the government to solve it and many felt that these systems were not doing their job properly.

In 2007–08, the year before my brother died, there were around 277 deaths from knives in England and Wales alone – this figure was the highest that had been recorded in thirty years. The legal age to buy a knife was still sixteen years old – not old enough to drive or drink or even vote, but old enough to own a lethal weapon. The penalty for carrying a knife was only a maximum of two years in prison and there was no minimum sentence – most people escaped with just a small fine or caution. In 2006, the then Home Secretary, John Reid, wanted to introduce tougher laws that would mean automatic jail sentences for carrying a weapon of up to five years. At the time of my brother's death two years later, these laws had still not been passed, although the penalty for carrying a knife had doubled to a maximum of four years and the legal age of owning one lifted to eighteen.

The legal definition of a dangerous knife is one that has a blade exceeding three inches; however, it only takes a stab wound of one inch deep to cut a main artery and kill someone, so this definition seems ridiculous. Apparently, switchblades and Swiss Army knives that have a blade smaller than three inches are perfectly legal, yet they are also the most accessible and therefore the most dangerous.

In 1996, 890 people were sentenced for possession of a knife in a public place – a figure that had increased to 6,284 ten years later.

It was clear that knife crime had been rising for a long time and that everybody thought the laws weren't tough enough to prevent it from rising further. Even the younger generation believed compulsory jail terms were necessary, with 57 per cent of sixteen to twenty-five-year-olds supporting this.

When I heard these statistics, I felt better about my opinions and it gave me a starting place to begin my fight. There were thousands of people writing to newspapers and calling television shows and demanding that the government pass laws that should have been introduced years ago. Yes, there were some who said it wouldn't make any difference, but surely it was worth a try?

The government had tried launching a knife amnesty, they had tried doubling the penalty, but were people being convicted and sentenced through this law? There's no point having a law if it's never used. When I did my research, I found that very, very rarely were people being given the maximum sentence – or any jail term for that matter – for carrying a knife.

When knife crime had first started to become a problem, had we then tried to talk to kids and rehabilitate them, we might not have got to where we were. Prevention is always better than cure, but we were at a point where we had almost reached an epidemic. Nearly every week, teenagers were losing their lives across the UK and softly-softly approaches weren't going to stop this quickly enough. We needed to scare kids enough to put down their weapons, we needed to put the power and authority back in the hands of the adults and the good people and we needed to do it now. Once some kind of order had resumed, maybe then we could think up long-term plans to reform and rehabilitate all those 'bad' kids, but until then we needed to concentrate on saving lives.

Finally, I had a basis for a plan of action and for once I felt I could honestly say what I felt. I sat down with my family and we wrote down what we wanted to see from our government and the people in authority, what actions we thought would make a difference so that someone else's child could live. The ideas seemed so obvious and we couldn't understand why none of them had already been put into practice. Had they been tried and simply not worked or had everybody just been too lazy?

We wanted all parents to receive a booklet on knife crime and the law and how it affects families. It seemed that many people didn't know what was legal and what wasn't, and were simply walking around carrying weapons because they thought it was allowed. If parents were reminded of the devastation doing this could cause, maybe they'd take more care ensuring their children weren't the ones walking about with knives. We wanted a new kind of Neighbourhood Watch to start up, with people caring about their community and identifying who

_____

might be a problem and feeling able to do something about it. Gone were the days where everybody looked after each other, now people were scared to even look outside their window – a fact that was proven when my brother was stabbed to death outside a busy pub and a residential estate and nobody came out to help him. I don't blame anybody for this – it's just a sad fact of life that we're all too scared to intervene. However, if people could build small teams in their communities where everybody was looking after each other, maybe confidence and protection would grow. Maybe people wouldn't be put in jail for standing up to thugs and would instead be commended for being heroes.

After parents and communities, we looked at schools, where kids spent nearly as much time as they did at home. Even in the 'well-behaved' secondary schools pupils were resorting to violence, and in the worst of the inner-city schools violence was all some of them knew. A child in a primary school in Northampton had recently threatened a classmate with a knife. What was going on out there when a child under the age of eleven was threatening the life of one of his fellow pupils? How had we come to this – a situation that would have been unimaginable twenty-five or thirty years ago? Granted, teachers didn't sign up to become classroom police officers but, nevertheless, their role is one of surrogate parents. Children are left in their care, and teachers know as much about every pupil as their parents, and sometimes even more. They know

_____

perfectly well early on who the troublesome kids are and they should be allowed to act on this information to ensure things don't get any worse. They should also be given sufficient search powers and, in the most extreme cases, schools that have suffered from knife crime should be provided with metal detectors at all entrances to reveal any hidden weapons. This sounds like a horrible environment for children to be in and it is sad that we should even have to consider such things, but I'm sure that most parents would rather their children were safe than comfortable, and if it got rid of just one weapon from one child it would be worth it.

Of course, these measures were easier said than done. Since the 1960s, and more so in recent years, teachers' powers of discipline have been stripped, and now they're unable to even raise their voices to a child, let alone enforce order. Children know their rights and are often backed up by their parents, stopping teachers from being able to do the good that they can.

We wanted ex-offenders and victims' families to go into schools and talk to kids and try to make them see what could happen if you went down the road of violence and weapons. They might not listen to their teachers, they might laugh at people they thought had nothing in common with them, but they might listen to somebody they believed had lived a life like theirs. If they could see how they'd turned out, maybe, just maybe, it would make them think.

———

Next we wanted to take the fight to a higher level. My brother had said that the police needed to be given more stop-and-search powers and that was one thing I wanted to bring into action. Many times I'd seen police attempting to search a group of teenagers on the streets, only to hear them laughing and saying, 'You can't touch me.' Thanks to legislation in the Human Rights Act, they were able to use these claims to their full advantage. We wanted the government to put more money into 'manpower' on the streets. I heard stories from my parents' generation of local policemen walking around the communities, forming relationships and trust with the people who lived in them. Today, there was no such relationship. Many people hated the police and didn't see any use for them, and this was down to a lack of effort on both sides. I believed that if police were given more stop-and-search powers, and indeed tools, such as metal-detecting wands, and were allowed to spend more time and effort in their local communities, then only good could come from it. It wouldn't change anything overnight – and it would indeed take a long time to change people's opinions and prejudices – but eventually people would begin to feel safer and would be thankful for it.

Finally, it was the government's turn. I was sick of politicans promising the world to us and then failing to deliver when they came into power. If anybody was immediately to blame for this problem, it was the Labour Party – they'd been in charge for years and were the only ones with power

———

to make changes immediately. If they had toughened the laws years ago, if they had focused more on youth and crime, things may not have gone this far.

There were many things I thought they could act on. From the extreme – compulsory and longer jail sentences, curfews for gangs and troublesome kids, fining parents if their children failed to comply with rules – to the more realistic and necessary solutions, most importantly by funding more youth clubs in all boroughs to provide safety and entertainment for kids on the street. This was a massive issue and nearly every kid I spoke to, whether they were 'good' or 'bad', complained that there was nothing else for them to do apart from hang around on the streets. If there was somewhere for them to go, a place that was regulated and provided them with shelter and fun activities, then I was sure the problem would begin to diminish. Interacting with other youths and taking part in team games and sports would also help children to develop the social skills they seemed to be lacking.

I also believed that we needed a nationwide advertising campaign that highlighted the problem. The government was still trying to sweep it under the carpet and pretend that we didn't have an epidemic and this wasn't good enough. There were also other minor but practical solutions like serving alcohol in plastic glasses in pubs and clubs frequented by young people, more funding to go into education – all things that would cost time and money but all things that could help us.

As well as all this, I was sure there was another answer out there, another way that could combine the necessary discipline with the rehabilitation idea – a national scheme that could be set up to stop these kids from becoming violent. I didn't know what form it might take yet, and I wasn't sure I could find anything that hadn't already been suggested, but I was determined to try. If people could put their heads together and come up with an idea that we could get the government to introduce that we could one day be proud of creating, I knew that I would at least feel I'd got some sort of justice for Ben and the countless others who were up there with him. With my demands written out, I set out on my journey. I decided I was going to start small and work my way up the chain of command to find out exactly what people were going to do about this problem. I would talk to parents, I would go into schools, I would work with the police and I would one day tackle the government and maybe even meet Prime Minister Brown himself to demand some answers.

Chapter 7

It's been three months since you died and I'm worried that I'm starting to forget you already. I feel so guilty for telling you that but it's true. When you were here I took you for granted – I didn't stop to look at your face any longer than necessary, I didn't always listen to your laugh and now I'm being punished because these precious memories are starting to fade.

If I close my eyes and concentrate, I can always bring you back in my head, but I know that I'm not doing you justice. I'm scared that my mind is changing your voice, your laugh, your face, and soon when I conjure you up, you won't even look like my brother any more. I look at every photo I have of you to calm me down, to help me remember, but then I get angry that all we have left of you are bits of paper.

I also feel guilty because I'm crying less. You are still the first thing I think of when I wake up and the last thing I picture when I try to go to sleep. You are still floating around my head every minute of every day, but lately I've found there are patches of time when I stop crying, when I find breathing easier, when I even dare to laugh.

The first time I really, properly laughed I hated myself. The first time my appetite came back and I ate something and actually enjoyed it I almost threw it back up. The first time I watched a programme and could almost concentrate on it without drifting off to think of you I wanted to die.

I have wanted to die since you did, Ben. We all have. We only voice it when we're in our lowest moments but, secretly, I know it crosses our minds all the time. I even made plans. I was seriously going to do it. I was just trying to find the right time and the right way so they wouldn't suffer any more heartbreak. I know they would have been angry with me but once everything had calmed down and they realized one of us was with you and that you were no longer on your own, I knew they'd feel better.

I held my plan like a precious jewel – it was the only thing that kept me going in those dark, early days. No matter how much it hurt, how much missing you made my heart break, it didn't matter because soon I would be back with you. I stopped wearing my seat belt, I drove recklessly, I walked down dark roads late at night praying to be attacked – I tempted fate as much as possible but it really didn't matter, as if God didn't help me I knew I'd do it myself.

Then one day I was out with Georgia, trying to cheer her up, make her smile. She hadn't smiled since she'd lost you, she'd hardly spoken; she just wandered around like a lost soul, a little sister without a big brother.

But this day, something stupid I said made her smile, and

then laugh – and that sound shocked me back into reality. I couldn't leave her too; that wouldn't be fair. She would still have Mummy and Daddy and Jade but what if they all decided to do the same thing, one by one, and she was left on her own – fourteen and abandoned. Or what if, God forbid, she copied me and tried to find us and didn't get to live the life she should? I needed to be there to give her advice and love and all the things big sisters give – and for the first time I wanted to do that. I wanted to give her all the things I should have been able to give you.

As soon as I realized I'd stopped wanting to kill myself, I felt a sense of guilt. Did this mean I'd stopped loving you? Had I chosen Georgia over you? Did the fact I could laugh and eat and seem happy mean that I was healed and that in three months I'd forgotten somebody I had adored for sixteen years?

Of course it didn't. Please believe me, Ben. I know you wouldn't have wanted me up there anyway – you're probably ruling the roost and don't need your big sister coming up to spoil the fun. I know you'd tell me that I need to be here and be strong and look after the rest of them, and that if I'd been silly enough to make my way up you would have probably kicked me back down.

I know all this but a tiny bit of my brain thinks: what if I'm wrong? What if you were really looking forward to it? What if you really are on your own and were so happy someone was coming for you and now they're not?

I will never know. I will never know where you are or how you feel until I see you again but I believe I know you well enough to know the truth. You won't let them take any more of us. *You'll be happy when you see us laughing and smiling. You'll be happy when, one day, we may just start feeling a little bit better. We will be happy, and it will be because of you.*

Joining in the fight against knife crime helped me a great deal. In the beginning, my solution to grief was simply to get as drunk as I could and cry myself to sleep, then start the process all over again the next day. It may seem from the way I speak that my family turned to alcohol a lot in the days after Ben's death but that wasn't the case and, in fact, I think we all did remarkably well considering the circumstances.

I was scared that when the grief really hit us we would all completely fall apart, slumping into depression and eventually hating each other. I read so many times that bereavement can cause parents to split up, cause families to resent and blame each other, and I couldn't bear it if this happened to us. We'd been such a close and loving family before Ben's death and it would be a terrible thing if not only did we lose him but we lost each other too.

I fully expected my mum and dad to be in the depths of despair over Ben's murder and wouldn't have blamed them if they had started drinking every day. I actually expected this to happen, not because they were alcoholics who dealt with all their problems like this, but because I knew they had to let their grief out in some way.

But they didn't. They continued being the amazing parents they always had been, and never once did they forget they still had four daughters and a son between them. My mum woke up early every single morning and sent Georgia safely off to school, she made sure her lunch was made and her clothes were clean, and she was always there to listen if Georgia came in and had had a bad day. She made sure we all ate properly and although, granted, we lived mainly on takeaways for the first few hard weeks, she was soon back to putting dinner on the table for us all. Our house was always clean, the pets always looked after – she didn't forget anybody. I was amazed at her strength. I expected days when she wouldn't even get out of bed but that didn't happen. Yes, she would have bad days where she'd break down and sob her heart out, and you never knew when they were coming – one minute she'd be smiling, the next bursting into tears – but this happened to us all. She dealt with her bad days by simply going off to have a 'nap', which was really a little cry, and then coming back down with her 'mum face' on.

When these bad days came, we all took ourselves off on our own to deal with them, none of us wanting to hurt each other even more. Maybe this was the only mistake we made – maybe we should have shared our grief more in the early days, spoken about Ben and how bad we were feeling, but it was hard to do that without feeling guilty for upsetting each other. Besides, we all knew that if we really needed to do that, one of us would always be there.

My dad was the same. He'd always been a quiet man but since Ben's death this had become even more evident.

He was always there for my mum and the rest of us, doing the shopping, attempting to cook dinner, trying to put a smile on, but you could tell it was even harder for him. Ben had been the only boy in the house and they'd had a close bond. Football games, computer matches, silly 'bloke' arguments – they shared things the rest of us didn't. I remember my dad saying that he missed the 'boy' things that used to lie around the house, even though he was constantly moaning at Ben to pick them up. He missed his little sidekick badly.

Also, I knew that my dad in some way blamed himself. He felt that he hadn't been there to protect his son that night and also felt that he hadn't done enough since. Everybody looks to their dad to solve their problems and sort out the bullies who come after us and we were no different. There had been countless times when boys had treated me badly and my dad had gone round there to 'have a little word'. Never in a violent or nasty way, simply in a way that said he was my dad and I was not to be messed with. This time, though, there was nothing he could do to make it better for any of us and you could tell it was eating him up.

The one major thing that did change was that my parents couldn't face going back to work. They had both worked so hard all their lives – before Ben died, my mum had been a secretary in a school, working the day shift, and my dad had been a London taxi driver, mainly working the nights. They made sure one of them was always there to look after us but worked as many hours as they could to support us. After Ben died, what began as a break from work while they were sorting things out turned into a permanent thing. My mum couldn't face working at the school where there were loads of kids her son's age around to remind her of him. It also went deeper than that. She practically became agoraphobic. She couldn't stand people or crowds, couldn't bear everyone asking how she was doing and if she was OK. Of course she wasn't. She preferred to stay cocooned in her house away from the whispers and the pitying stares, and my dad was the same.

He also had another problem to deal with. As a taxi driver, there were many times that he had rowdy and drunk passengers in his cab – sometimes the worst they did was throw up on his back seat but often they would dodge the fare and run, leaving him with no money for his efforts. Sometimes they even turned violent and this is what scared us the most. My dad was angry enough as it was – all he needed was a confrontation or an excuse to set him off and who knew what the consequences would be? Therefore, they both stayed safely tucked away, though naturally this also added to their problems. Lack of money, too much time together, too much time to think – it all added to their grief. It's these small things, these changes to your life that people don't get to hear about or under-stand. Many people told them to get back to work – that it would help them, keep them busy, get them motivated. It's not as simple as that. It's hard to get up most days, let alone go out to face the world and earn a living. Losing somebody in this way had a ripple effect and it affected us all in every single aspect of our lives.

My sisters each dealt with their grief in their own way. Jade had always been a party animal and it seemed this environment was the best outlet for her. She went out with friends who took care of her and found that being away from the house and the sadness was, for her, much easier. In the beginning, I resented her for this. I thought she was simply out getting drunk all the time, not caring about any of us and not doing her share of looking after everybody. Then one day I reminded myself that she was still only twenty-two and didn't know what else to do. She'd been so close to Ben – it was Jade who'd take him out for a little dance or a beer, have special in-jokes with him . . . and it was Jade who'd got the original phone call that he'd been stabbed. It was a lot for a young girl to deal with and so I let her get on with it the best way she knew how, only wishing sometimes that I could join her, let myself go and stop worrying about everything.

Georgia was the quietest and the hardest to help. She'd always been hard to figure out – a typical teenage girl who was just hitting puberty, she'd been withdrawn and quiet even before this had happened to Ben. The only person who could bring her out of her shell had been Ben and they were always to be found in one of their bedrooms, heads bent together, gossiping quietly and laughing loudly.

She tried her hardest not to show how sad she was and although we begged her to talk to us, she wouldn't, or simply couldn't. We asked her to go to counselling and, to give her credit, she did try, but she couldn't seem to find the words she wanted to say. Instead she started boxing and we hoped that this would let out some of her frustration and anger. As she was eating, sleeping and socializing, we decided she was doing as well as she could and let her get on with things, though obviously we kept a close eye on her.

I handled things very differently. After the initial period of getting drunk and lying in bed, I acknowledged that wasn't helping me at all. When I read Ben's school work that day and finally realized I had a plan of action, I threw myself into it and found that keeping myself busy was the cure I'd been looking for.

There was nothing I wouldn't do. Every show that asked, every paper that wanted an interview, everyone who wanted me to talk to them, I agreed. I know some people thought that I was simply doing it for the publicity, trying to get my name back in the public eye, but I really wasn't. I visited schools where there were no press at all to watch me and report, and spoke to kids from the bottom of my heart. I simply wanted to do all I could to get my campaign going and also wanted to distract myself as much as possible. I didn't want to give myself one minute to think, one minute to remember the pain.

Why Ben?

When the media started to hear I was going on my journey, they all wanted to document it in some way. Papers wanted to print a diary, television companies wanted to make a documentary – I couldn't believe how many people were interested in Ben's story.

However, I was still really reluctant. I'd decided to go on this personal journey for myself and my family. I didn't want people thinking it was just so I could get more work as an actress or a presenter or just so that I could look like some kind of saint or hero. I was only doing it so I could get my questions answered and get the right people to admit blame for what had happened to our streets and make some changes. I soon found out, though, that the best way to make these people sit up and listen was to get as many people behind me as possible, and that the best way to do that was to show as many people as I could what I was doing.

I finally decided to make a documentary along the way. I'd seen many documentaries on serious, factual subjects – emotional ones, distressing ones, honest and real ones – and they always got straight to my heart and affected me. I wanted to do something like that. I wanted to tell our story in a way that didn't ask for pity, didn't pressure people to feel bad or sorry for us, but simply told the facts about knife crime and the possible solutions – if and when I found them out myself.

There were quite a few production companies who made offers but I was adamant I didn't want to do an

'MTV' reality-type documentary. I didn't want them to follow me and my family around crying and wailing – in fact, I didn't want my family on it at all. They'd never wanted to be in the limelight and, unless they chose to be, I wasn't going to force them to do something like this.

I wanted a team who'd let me do the things I needed to, who'd let me follow the avenues I wanted and who'd help me get to the people I needed to reach. I wanted people I could trust and who wouldn't try to make me seem like somebody I wasn't, as the most important thing I wanted to get across to the public was that I had absolutely no idea how to go about solving the problem. I was willing to learn, I was willing to fight, but at the moment I didn't know how. I didn't want to be airbrushed, I didn't want to have answers whispered in my ears and fake meetings set up – I just wanted to be real and honest.

I finally found the company I thought was right. They were called Steadfast and I agreed to make a one-off documentary with them for the BBC. I would allow them to film me over the course of the next year. This seemed fitting to me, as the BBC was where I'd spent most of my career and I knew it was one of the most well-respected and popular channels. I worried whether I was doing the right thing but all of a sudden the choice had been made, the contract had been signed and I was on my way. I agreed to let the TV crew film me whenever I was doing something relating to knife crime and my campaign (and only if it was appropriate) and, in return, they agreed to set up meetings and interviews with people I needed to talk to. They would follow me up until Ben's trial and the documentary would culminate with the verdict and (hopefully) the subsequent sentencing. We had quite a few months to go until then, though, and a lot to get through.

One of the first things I remember doing as part of my work and the documentary was the *News of the World*'s Save Our Streets campaign. They had organized a fantastic campaign, travelling from city to city across the country and asking panel members, such as MPs, police officers and youth workers, to come and talk to the public and answer their questions and concerns on knife and gun crime. They visited every major city that had been affected by this horrific problem and asked families of children who'd been lost to violence to come along and talk about their experiences and demand some answers from the people in authority.

It seemed like a fitting place to start my own journey. I'd wanted to speak to those in charge, as well as to families and to the public, and here was my chance. I was asked to attend the last road show in London and was also honoured when I was asked to be a panel member. I had just expected to be sitting in the crowd with other victims and members of the public but they wanted me on the panel so people could ask about the work I'd been doing and what I planned to do next.

I decided to take my dad along for moral support and by the time we arrived I was shaking. If you put a script in my hand and ask me to perform I'm fine, as I've dealt with scripts throughout my career, but if you put a camera on me and ask me to just be me, I don't know what to do. It was scary enough that I was going to have to face members of the public and answer questions, but I was also going to be filmed doing so. However, this was all my choice and I had no one to blame but myself. There was no backing out now.

The event was held in a big conference hall. The table for the panel was in the centre of the hall, with the audience seats sloping upwards. As I took my seat and stared up at the audience sitting above me, it felt like I was in a lion's den. Suddenly I wasn't sure if I was on the right side of the table. However, I caught my dad's face in the audience and felt reassured.

I was right to have fears about being on that panel. Although it was a great privilege and was always going to be hard because it was one of the first public things I'd done, I felt I was seen as an ally of the other people on that panel and, as I quickly realized, in the eyes of the audience some of them were very unpopular, so at times I felt like I too was being attacked.

I was on the panel with many powerful professionals, including His Honour Gerald Butler (a former judge), Iain Duncan Smith (former leader of the Conservative Party), Sir Paul Stephenson (the Deputy Metropolitan Police Commissioner) and Shaun Bailey (a youth worker). Members of the public were angry with some of these people as they represented systems they felt had let them down. Although I could see where they were coming from, I also felt slightly sorry for my fellow panel members. They weren't the only ones responsible for the problem and at least they'd had the decency to come along and contribute.

The most awful thing about that day was listening to the heartbreaking stories. When Ben was murdered, it was such a shock and such an unnatural thing that it seemed as if my family were the only people in the world who'd ever gone through it. Obviously we knew better and we knew that this was happening every day, but when your world is ripped apart, it feels like no one will ever understand. However, here I was listening to person after person telling their own stories – mum after mum, dad after dad crying at how they had lost their children to unnecessary violence. I couldn't believe how many people were hurting. Some cried, some shouted, some spoke positive messages that made the audience cheer and made me shake my head in astonishment. How could they take something so horrific and use it to make something better? How could they not be bitter about what had happened?

I wasn't actually asked many questions. The audience was gunning for the people in charge and I wasn't important enough. I remember one woman asking me why my brother had got so much attention, why he was any different from anybody else when her own son had also died that way, and although it was the only question I had been asked, I couldn't answer. It was my worst nightmare, it was the question I'd been dreading and I completely froze. I don't even remember what I said. I tried to tell them that I was doing this for all the kids and that I was amazed by the courage and spirit I'd seen that day but I don't think I came across very well. I could feel tears welling in my eyes and simply sat there, feeling ashamed and wanting it to be over.

Finally, when everybody had had their say and the anger was vented, it was finished. I walked over to where my dad was waiting to give me a hug and burst into tears. It had been so emotional and tough and I wasn't sure I could take it. My first mission and I had fallen apart already. However, that day toughened me up. It made me realize that not everybody was going to like me, not everybody would agree with me and my ideas, and that they didn't have to. They had the right to their own opinions and feelings and, rather than get upset, all I could do was carry on with my plan and take strength from the people who were behind me.

Listening to those families talk about their experiences was so hard but it taught me something. The desperation and anger in their voices was not only for the loss of their children but because they were sick of nobody listening to them. All they wanted was to talk about the child they'd lost, and find out why and give ideas of their own, yet nobody was willing to listen. I could see the frustration in their eyes and hear the rage in their voices when they demanded to know why this had happened, yet all they kept being told was – we don't know, it wasn't our fault.

I knew that the families of the victims were the best people to talk to. Having gone through this myself, I knew that nobody else could guess at the pain it caused, nobody could put themselves in your shoes and imagine what it was like. People did try, and we were grateful, but if I heard 'I understand' or 'He's in a better place now' or 'It was his destiny' one more time I would scream.

It *wasn't* his fate, it *wasn't* the way his life was meant to go – he simply didn't have a choice.

The government and police could call in all the 'experts' they wanted – they could talk to social workers and doctors and psychiatrists, but if they wanted a well-rounded view, if they wanted to know the devastation and cracks this problem really caused, they needed to speak to us – the ones left behind.

I asked my documentary people to see if there were any other families who'd been through this who would be willing to meet with me. I wanted to meet a few who were at different stages along the way of this nightmare. I wanted to ask someone who'd suffered this for months or years and see how they were coping, if they were coping, if they could tell me how to cope.

I also wanted to meet somebody that this was all new to as well. Friends and family were great at helping and trying to understand but we couldn't put into words how hard it was to lose Ben. I wanted to speak to a family like ours and see if they found it as tough – ultimately, I knew that they would understand and that maybe I would finally have somebody to talk to.

Chapter 8

A couple of weeks before you died, you were certain you'd seen a ghost. I wasn't there the next morning when you came down, pale and shaken, but Mummy told me later.

You were in your bed asleep and, for no reason at all, you woke up in the middle of the night. You said that instantly you knew something was wrong, you knew there was somebody in the room with you.

You didn't know how you knew this but you could tell. You peeped out from under your covers and in front of you was the ghost of an old lady just standing there staring at you. She looked at you for a few seconds and then turned and walked into your wardrobe.

You nearly burst into tears but simply grabbed the dog, who like always was sleeping with you, clung onto him and hid under the covers until morning.

When Mummy laughed at you and asked why you didn't call

for her or come and wake her up, you said you couldn't – you said you were absolutely frozen.

I spoke to you about it later and by then you'd calmed down and were laughing about it but you didn't dismiss it. You knew it wasn't just a dream; you knew you had seen that ghost.

I didn't dismiss it either. I believed you with all my heart. Especially now, with what's happened. All these little things, these funny signs, make me wonder if your course was set in stone. Did that ghost lady come to check up on you, did she come to meet you to prepare you for what lay ahead? Was that ghost lady death itself?

I am petrified of ghosts. I've never seen one and never wanted too. We'd watch scary films together, you and me, both of us huddling under the covers, and I'd declare that if I ever saw a ghost I would have a heart attack on the spot.

But it's different now. Now, I pray every night that I will see a ghost and that the ghost will be you. Even if it's a different ghost, at least I'd have hope that they exist and that one day you'll be able to come too. Don't think you'll scare me, Ben. I promise you, you won't. I'm braver now and would risk having a heart attack just to see you.

I hope that you've met that old lady again and that she's explained to you what she was doing that night and said sorry for scaring you. I hope that she's shown you the way to get back and visit and if she doesn't, you tell her she'll have me to answer to.

I picture you as a ghost and can't help but laugh. I know how much fun you'd have playing tricks, teasing people, tormenting all those who annoyed you over the years. I don't want to interrupt your fun but if you could find the time to visit, even if it is just to play a joke, I really would appreciate it.

When I started meeting other families, the first person I was introduced to was a man named Mark Prince. His son Kiyan had been stabbed to death in May 2006, over two years earlier. He had been a budding footballer who played for the Queen's Park Rangers youth team. He was described as an outstanding and lovely boy by all who knew him and his life was ended at half past three in the afternoon following an altercation in which it was said he was sticking up for another boy who was being bullied.

Mark Prince was amazing. When he walked into the café where I sat waiting for him I didn't know what to think. He was a tall, very well-built black man with shiny gold teeth, wearing an iPod round his neck and singing along loudly. He didn't say a word to me until he'd finished humming his song and then he smiled a big, wide smile, grabbed my hand in his massive one and pulled me into a hug.

He automatically demanded some food from the crew and then sat down confidently and asked me what I needed.

If ever there was a person made to be a role model for this sort of thing, it would be Mark Prince. At first I was absolutely petrified of him – I had never met anybody like him before. On first impressions, you might have thought he was quite scary himself from the intimidating attitude he exuded, but when he opened his mouth and began to talk, that prejudice was completely blown away.

He spoke so softly that you had to strain to hear what he was saying, and strain I did because I didn't want to miss a word. He told me about his beautiful Kiyan and what it had been like for the past couple of years for him and the rest of his children.

What amazed me was that he wasn't bitter or angry any more. In a few years he had changed his opinion of what had happened and wanted to make sure it didn't happen again. Unlike me, he didn't really agree with stricter sentences or tougher jails, he wanted rehabilitation and programmes for the kids on the streets, and he had some great ideas in mind.

Just as I thought, he was frustrated because nobody had listened to him so far and when he told me his idea for a community programme, I couldn't understand why they hadn't. It was brilliant and the more he talked, the more I became swayed and started thinking, maybe this is the way forward? We had a great debate where we both stated our opinions on the solution and he never made me feel bad or wrong, he just smiled and came back at me with a different answer.

What completely astounded me about Mark is that he had decided to forgive his son's killer. He even wanted to meet him in the near future to look into his eyes and talk about what had happened and why. I could understand this, as it was what I also wanted to do one day, but I was sure I wouldn't be doing it in the calm, forgiving way Mark had planned.

He believed this was essential for the grief process and also for restorative justice for both the victim and the offender, where they had to face up to their actions. I wasn't sure if his idea would ever work – I believed that introducing victim's families to offenders would probably result in a lot more casualties – but I commended him for his strong beliefs. I worried that maybe he was a better person than me because he felt like this but again he told me to find my own path. He reminded me that I was just starting out on this journey and that he had been exactly the same as me in the beginning, but even angrier. He told me to take my time and that maybe one day, I would have the same views as he did. I couldn't ever imagine forgiving my brother's killers but didn't want to ruin his hope and so I thanked him for his time and we promised we'd stay in touch and help each other if needed. We've done so ever since and Mark has become a good friend.

When I left, he lectured me to take care of myself, to eat properly, drink water and get lots of exercise. He told me to go running every day to get my mind and health working properly and I laughed at him, as this was the last thing I wanted to do. I didn't care about my health any more – what was the point when you could lose it all tomorrow?

He told me off sternly and said if I didn't look after

myself, I couldn't look after anybody else and therefore would be useless. I could see the amazing dad he was. My heart broke that Kiyan had missed out on this man and his teachings. He still drives me mad now, asking me if I'm taking care of myself and, although maybe I bend the truth and exaggerate a little bit, he has inspired me to at least try.

Meeting Mark made me confused. He put such good arguments across for rehabilitation instead of punishment and although I wanted to believe that was the answer to everything, I simply couldn't. It still didn't seem fair to help these people when they had done such wrong. Maybe I was being too stubborn or selfish but I wasn't able to accept this was the best way. I felt I would be letting my brother down and betraying him.

The next man I met was called Sal Idriss. His brother Nass Osawe was killed months before my brother in Islington, where we lived. I remember reading about it and being horrified that something like this had happened in my community again. There had already been a well-publicized stabbing of a boy called Martin Dinnegan the year before and when it happened again everybody was shocked.

Nass had been at a bus stop with a couple of friends two days after Christmas and had got into an altercation with another boy and his dog, who alleged the group were laughing and 'looking' at him. The boy then stabbed one of Nass's friends and, when they chased him away, fatally stabbed Nass twice with a blade just one and a half inches long. Although his killer received a life sentence, again he was only given the minimum of twelve years to serve before being eligible for parole.

I met his brother Sal about eight months after Nass had died and although he was only a few months ahead of me along the process, I was amazed at how strong he also seemed. He told me his family were still completely devastated and were having a hard time getting through it, but that he had decided to do something constructive to try and make a difference. Using his skill as a photographer, he wanted to stage an exhibition to highlight knife crime and get everybody talking about it. He wanted to shock people into doing something and his idea was to ask as many families as possible who'd lost someone to knife or gun crime to take part. His intention was to present the devastated families honestly. Not as names, numbers or headlines, that eventually disappear, but as families who are coping with loss, pain and immense sadness every day for the rest of their lives. One of his ideas to truly reflect the horror and grief of the families involved was to take them back to the place where their loved ones were murdered.

I didn't know what to say to this. It sounded so controversial and hard-hitting, and I wasn't sure how the public would take to it but, like me, Sal was tired of tiptoeing around. He wanted people to wake up and really see what was going on, rather than brushing it under the carpet, and he thought using tactics like this was the only way to get the message across. I agreed with him on this but when he asked if my family and I would help him and take part, I froze. Although I thought it was a good, original idea and wanted to help him, I couldn't imagine taking my family back to where Ben had been attacked and stand there posing for photos so soon after his death. I gently told Sal this and said that he might have the same problem with a lot of the families, as it would be such an emotional thing to do. I felt so guilty saying I couldn't help him because he'd given up his time to meet me but he told me not to worry. He knew it was going to be a struggle but he was determined to try and I really hoped he succeeded.

When I met Sal, I fully expected that as Nass's older brother he'd still be in the depths of depression and unable to focus on anything. When I told him I admired him, he said he felt the same about me, but I didn't understand. I didn't feel I was doing anything spectacular, I was just trying to pass on Ben's legacy. I was more amazed by the other members of the family, the people like my mum and dad who were still holding the fort together at home. It struck me then that maybe we were all doing this because we had no other choice. When the thought ever crossed my mind that one day I might lose somebody I loved, I always pictured not being able to go on, not having the strength to live any more. But here I was, meeting families who were all surviving the best they could. I think that, as humans, we are incapable of doing anything else but trying to survive and even when the worst thing in the world happens to you, you still try your best to muddle through.

I met many other families – the Mizens, the Knoxes and others – who were all equally wonderful and whom I stay in touch with regularly. We all supported each other through our trials, as all our loved ones were lost within weeks of each other. On special occasions we would text each other and, although none of us had known the other kids who'd been killed, it felt like we had. It was nice to have people to talk to and although all of these people became some kind of friend or support to me over those months, the person I bonded most with was, unexpectedly, Richard Taylor, father of Damilola.

Richard had attended my brother's funeral, unbeknown to me or my family, before I'd ever even met him. I was told this later and was very grateful but didn't think I'd ever see him again. I remember Damilola's case very well – as will most of the nation, as nobody can forget that smiling ten-year-old boy who was brutally murdered in November 2000.

What I didn't realize was that in the past eight years, Richard had been fighting every day for some sort of change. He'd set up a youth centre in memory of his son, he'd campaigned avidly and even though he'd lost his wife in early 2008, he still didn't let anything set him back.

I started running into him at different events and charity nights and people would always introduce us. Slowly, despite our age and cultural differences, we built up a friendship and I began to see just how respected by everybody he was.

He also spoke of change – he wanted more youth centres built, more things for kids to do, more rewards for those kids who were behaving themselves and making a difference. Out of everybody, I felt that he was the one who most understood my point of view, as that was what I wanted too. His ideas were similar to mine and he was determined not to stop until he'd got a result.

He once told me an amazing story about Damilola. When he was younger, before he had come to England, he'd been playing outside when a shaman, someone who is thought to see the future, had told Damilola that he would one day be stabbed. Damilola was distraught and ran crying to his dad, who promptly went and told the shaman off.

Shortly after, Damilola came to England to gain a better education and life, but sadly never got the chance because the awful prophecy came true.

Richard told me he hadn't told many people this story, and I hope he doesn't mind me relating it now, but it struck me how similar it was to my own brother's prediction in his writing. Damilola also loved to write and even at his very young age composed beautiful poetry. The amazing prose he wrote, which is inscribed on the wall of his youth centre, is wonderful and has stayed with me ever since I heard it.

Why Ben?

I will travel far and wide to choose my destiny to remould the world. I know it is my destiny to defend the world, which I hope to achieve in my lifetime.

A little while after I first met Richard, we were asked to do something spectacular together. A few months after Ben had died, the furore over knife crime was reaching a high. Everyone was talking about it, everyone wanted to do something about it and the government had finally started to wake up and listen to us.

In May 2008, just before Ben died, a huge police operation named Operation Blunt 2 was launched. Its sole purpose was to fight knife crime and they would attempt to do this by sending officers out to patrol the streets of London every night, performing stop and searches and promoting safety in the communities. Although this was already up and running by the time Ben was murdered, the press coverage of his death and the many others who died after him seemed to highlight the issue even more. The government increased their efforts, reassuring the public that both they and the police force would be putting even more funding and resources into the problem. The government also demanded that all hospitals now had to report any stabbings – something that hadn't previously been compulsory but was vital in finding out the true statistics of this problem.

Although the Home Office had previously run anti-knife crime advertising, the public had deemed them 'not shocking enough' so a few months later new material was produced which they hoped would be more effective. Shortly after Ben's death, they produced a booklet to go into schools which advised people about knife crime and the law and likely punishment.

All these changes and improvements were great and were exactly what I had wanted and written down in my list of demands, but it still wasn't enough.

We still had to unite everybody and make them feel a part of the solution and not the problem – we had to show the people out there who were still doing this that they were the minority and that the majority had had enough and were now willing to put a stop to them.

In September 2008, two young girls, Sharon Singh and Gemma Olway, had an amazing idea and wanted to try something that had never been done before.

They planned a march against knife and gun crime, starting from both the north and south of London and marching for a few hours all through central London where people would meet up together, before going on to a rally at Hyde Park.

It was a massive feat and took a lot of planning but they were backed by the *Daily Mirror* newspaper, which publicized the march every day, and it soon gathered momentum. Shortly before the actual day of the march, I was asked to lead the people going from the north, and was told that Richard Taylor would be leading the south. This was to symbolize the joining of forces, the tolerance of other people from different areas. There'd been so much talk of gangs fighting because of different postcodes and 'turf wars' and if we could get these two areas, notorious for disliking each other, to come together as one it would be a massive accomplishment.

I felt privileged to be asked to lead the march and on the day went down to the starting point with most of my family. Just like Ben's march, there was a great turnout of people, all with placards and banners, all excited, all ready to make a stand. There were babies, kids, teenagers – all wearing T-shirts of loved ones; it was a wonderful sight. We started off and, although it was late September, the sun shone all day, making it hard to keep going in the heat. However, nobody complained or gave up – they simply marched along, chanting and singing songs. There were choirs, rappers, religious chants – everybody shouted at the tops of their voices for people to lay down their weapons.

Finally, I was told we were nearing the meeting point. The news travelled back and everybody began to get excited. The atmosphere changed and I really felt like I was a part of something monumental.

At last, we saw the southern side marching towards us in the distance. Both sides began cheering and clapping, but nobody ran or got out of hand. We continued walking towards each other and finally Richard was a few steps in front of me, with everybody waiting.

I was really shy and didn't know what to do – this was

such a symbolic thing and I didn't want to ruin it, but nobody had told me what I was supposed to do. Richard solved it by stepping forward and hugging me and then everybody went crazy. People were shouting and cheering and crying and the press surrounded us, trying to capture the moment on film. I clung on to Richard, unable to move for fright, but eventually, the crowds were closing in on us too much and I couldn't breathe until I was finally pulled away.

I can't do justice to that moment in words. When I first heard the idea I thought it was good, but never thought it would have the impact it did. It was an event that would go down in history, all down to the work of two girls who had never been personally affected by knife crime but who just wanted to make a difference.

We all continued to Hyde Park, where there was a rally, complete with singers, motivational speakers, messages from celebrities and families and even Prime Minister Gordon Brown himself.

At one point they got all the families on stage while a choir sang Take That's 'We Can Rule the World'. There were many, many tears; however when I look at the photos, I'm horrified because it looks like I'm laughing. The reason for this is that when my dad walked on stage, he started waving and wouldn't stop. I thought he was waving to the crowds and asked him whether he thought he was the Queen or something, but he was actually waving to my mum, who hadn't been strong enough to come. He was hoping the TV cameras would catch him and she'd see him and that really made me smile.

The whole day was beautiful and it really marked a change in the way people were thinking. I was finally getting somewhere on my journey now. I'd listened to other people's opinions, and we'd highlighted issues and had influenced policy-makers. However, now that people had started to notice the work I was doing, they were also starting to ask me what I thought the solution was, what I was suggesting we do? I still wasn't sure, but it was time to put what I had learned into practice and go and find out.

Before I could do that, though, there was a big ordeal to get through. I had almost forgotten that me and my family had another journey to go on, another hurdle to get through – the reason I'd been doing all this in the first place.

Chapter 9

I had my first dream about you last night. I have prayed and prayed every night for you to come and visit me, for you to just let me know that you are OK, but you haven't yet. I read once that when somebody is badly hurt and killed, they have to spend some time in heaven healing all their wounds, so maybe that's what you're doing. Or maybe you're just having too much fun up there to come and see your big sis.

It wasn't a very nice dream but it was still so wonderful to see your familiar face. You haven't changed one bit. I knew that you wouldn't have because you are in my mind, in my memory, where you will stay the same forever, frozen at sixteen, but I was worried you would look different, wouldn't look like my Ben.

In the dream you'd played a practical joke on a group of men. They were angry with you and so they decided to punish you. You had to stand outside a room while me, Mummy and Jade waited with you. They had drawn horizontal lines all up your leg, starting from your ankle and working their way up through your new tattoo. You had to wait outside the door until they called you in.

I could tell you were petrified but you kept smiling so we wouldn't get upset. It didn't stop us though. We were all sobbing and begging you not to go into the room but you just smiled and said you had to. 'It will be over soon,' you kept saying. Finally they called you into the room and when the door opened we could only see darkness before it shut again. We heard a shout and then we heard you cry and then the door opened and you limped out. When you turned around, we saw they'd sliced open one of the lines on your leg, and blood was dripping down. You just smiled bravely and said it didn't hurt, and waited for them to call you in again.

This happened over and over again and every time I tried to wake up, tried to save us both from the pain, but I couldn't. I had to see what happened in the end. Finally, they told you it was the last time. They had worked their way up to the last line. You looked relieved and we hugged you before you went in and waited impatiently for you to come out so we could take you home. The door opened for the last time and you came out with a sad look on your face and you smiled as I reached for you, but before I could grab you, a hand came out and in that hand was a knife – a knife that already had your blood on it and it reached up and stabbed you in the heart. Before I could catch you as you fell, I woke up crying.

As painful and horrific as this dream was, I wanted to go back. I closed my eyes and begged sleep to take me back to that place, to take me back to you because I couldn't bear to think of you alone there in the nightmare. Of course I knew it wasn't real, that that wasn't how it had happened, but if I could only get back and change things, stop you going through that door one last time, everything would be OK.

I didn't go back to sleep. I spent the whole day crying and that night I was scared to go to sleep in case I had that dream again. But I didn't. I had a different one. Again you came to visit me – only quickly, but it was enough. It was me and you on our own in the desert and you were lying in the sand and I had to cover you up in a black bag. As I got to your face, I cried and said I didn't want to do it but you smiled that lovely, big smile again and told me that I had to, and told me not to worry, and told me you were going to be OK.

You haven't been to see me since. I don't know why you had to give me such horrible dreams. I don't know why you couldn't have taken me to the fair or the seaside or somewhere nice, but I do know that somehow, you found a way to come and visit me. You found a way to tell me you were OK.

On 13 October 2008, I saw the three men that had been accused of murdering my brother for the first time. Not just in person, but ever. No photos of the accused had been published before the trial so I had no idea what any of them looked like. All I knew were their names and their ages.

I had pictured them in my head only a few times, but I rarely let myself think about them, not wanting to waste any more of my life on them than I had to, and also scared that the anger and rage I had kept at a distance so far would come rushing out if I thought about them too much.

However, when you live in an area like I do, there are always rumours and gossip floating around. People would try to tell us things about them, would claim that they knew them or had heard of their reputations, would state they had played football with one of them only the other week like a sick boast – all things we didn't want to hear, things we didn't care about.

It turned out that I even knew the sister of one of them. When I was a teenager, I'd spent some time hanging around on the estate near where Ben was killed. This was only for a couple of years but I knew quite a few of the people who lived there and although I hadn't been back there in ten years, I thought I still had enough friends there to mean nothing would ever happen to me or anyone I loved. Of course, nobody around there knew my brother – he'd never set foot on that estate or anywhere near it – but it was still a blow to find out he'd been murdered so near to where I grew up and knew people.

When we first heard the names of the accused, they meant nothing to me. Although one of them lived on that estate I'd never come across him and as the other two didn't live in my area, they were strangers too. So it was a shock when I realized I knew the sister of one of them – not well, not as a friend or even a casual acquaintance, but I knew of her. I knew what she looked like, I had even spoken to her once or twice all those years ago. I felt that it connected me to this family in some way and I didn't like it. I didn't want to know any of them, I wanted them to remain the evil strangers they were. I thought that if I was even remotely connected to one of them, even if it was just through a family member, there could be some rhyme or reason as to why they'd chosen my brother and I knew this wasn't the case at all. They had just chosen the easiest target.

When I pictured my brother's killers, all I saw were monsters – real-life, terrifying monsters. Men who were ten feet tall, with grotesque, deformed faces and powerful muscles. Men who had knives the size of swords and evil in their hearts. Your mind exaggerates these things and makes you panic and although I wanted to see the accused to put my mind at rest, to stop having the horrific nightmares, I wasn't ready yet. I wasn't strong enough.

The plea hearing for the trial was held on 13 October. It was a formal hearing where the defendants stated whether they were pleading guilty or not guilty and their teams went through paperwork, formalities and so on. The whole thing would last less than an hour and the police told us there was no need for us to be there, that it wasn't anything we needed to bother with.

But of course we did. To us it was the most important day of all, the day when the accused could own up and admit what they'd done. We'd been warned that that wasn't going to happen, that all of them would plead not guilty as murder has a compulsory life sentence, which meant people rarely pleaded guilty to it, even if there was no way they would be acquitted. They would plead not guilty and take the chance their lawyers would get them off – and in this day and age there was more than a slim chance of that happening.

My parents were adamant they wanted to be there and although I wanted to go along and support them, because I knew there would be press and because I knew it would be upsetting, I really didn't want to see those men. We all had different feelings and emotions about them. My sisters and my dad would probably want to be locked in a room with them if they had the chance, my mum wanted to look them in the eye and see justice done for her son, but I couldn't bear to be near them. For a start, I was scared I would show weakness and break down crying, but most importantly, I couldn't stand looking into the last faces Ben had possibly seen. If they looked as scary as I'd imagined, I didn't know what I'd do or if my mind and heart could cope.

Some of my family had seen the accused once before. Days after Ben was murdered and the three men had finally been caught, they attended our local court to watch them being officially charged. Although I wanted to go, I was petrified and in the end, my parents and my sisters Holly and Jade went while I stayed at home with Georgia. When they came back, their faces were pale and they could barely contain their rage. Jade tried to describe what the men looked like but I couldn't picture them in my head, I couldn't get rid of the monsters. To make things worse, friends of theirs had been hanging around inside and outside the court – boys in hoodies and caps, girls who gave dirty looks. They were intimidating and my family were made to feel like *they* were the bad ones, like *they* were the criminals.

Strangely enough, not one of their family members seemed to be there that day. No mums, no dads, no one responsible for the people these men had become. I don't know whether they were told to stay away by the police or whether they just couldn't face it, but I found it strange that the only people who turned up were their thuggish friends. If Ben had been accused of murdering someone, I'm sure my parents would have been there wanting to find out the truth.

Since Ben died, I've often wondered, what if it had been *him* accused of stabbing somebody? If Ben had turned out to be one of those kids who carried a weapon, and if on the day he'd been attacked he'd used it and killed somebody, how would we, his family, feel? I knew the answer immediately. Even if it was self-defence, we would tell him he was wrong. If he had caused the devastation to another family that had been caused to ours, we would want him to pay for it and to be punished. Yes, we would still love him; no, we wouldn't shut him out of our lives and forget he existed, forget the shame and guilt he'd brought down on us, but we would urge him to tell the truth, to stand up and admit what he'd done and to quietly get on with the sentence he deserved.

However, in real life, Ben hadn't been killed through an act of self-defence. It was three on one, it was unnecessary and there was no need for it to happen – he hadn't done anything wrong. I could understand that the defendants' families would still love them no matter what, for I knew any good parent should, but I couldn't understand why they weren't telling them to do the right thing. Of course, at this time, it's easy to say they might have all been innocent, that maybe they'd also done nothing wrong, but my brother didn't die of his own accord. Those men had been named and charged; there was evidence they had been there that night; they had to give us some answers.

A couple of days before the plea hearing, the police told us that the defendants would probably not be attending court that day. They said they might appear on video link to give their pleas or they might not even do that, but instead get their lawyers to do the talking for them.

Although I was disgusted that they didn't even have to turn up to answer for themselves, I was also relieved, as at least I could now go to court with my parents and support them without worrying. Jade couldn't go on that day as she had work and Georgia was too young, so in the end me, my mum and my dad got ready to start Ben's journey to justice.

On the morning of the hearing, we woke up with our stomachs churning. None of us could eat, we could barely get dressed and we were all shaking. We knew what was probably going to happen and that there wouldn't be any big revelations or discoveries but we still couldn't squash the hope that maybe one of them would change their minds and plead guilty. Maybe one of them would do the right thing and put us out of this misery.

I remember not knowing what to wear. I'd performed jury service a couple of years ago but apart from that I'd never been to court and, although it wasn't the case, I felt like we were on trial. If we turned up messy and unkempt, would that affect the way the judge saw our family? Would it affect the way he saw Ben?

I borrowed some of Jade's work clothes and felt like a kid playing dress-up. I came down and my mum was dressed almost identically, which made us both laugh at least.

We made our way to the Old Bailey, which was where all the big, serious cases are tried. Before we went in, we met up with the head detective on the case and our family liaison officers and they gave us a quick briefing.

Before Ben died, I hadn't had any dealings with the police, and knew nothing about how they operated, but by now I felt I could probably be one of them myself. I'd never had any opinion either way about them. As a kid, I regarded them as strict and there simply to frighten everyone and keep some kind of order. I'd grown up with friends who would do naughty things and, when they were caught by the police, would moan that all they did was ruin people's fun and waste time on small crimes while ignoring the big ones.

However, since Ben's death, the police had been one of our biggest supports. Everybody from the local police to the team that had been brought in and put in charge of his case was amazing and you could see that they really wanted to see justice for Ben.

We'd been given two family liaison officers in the early days named Steve and Mandy. They were basically the middlemen between my family and the investigative team but they became much more than that. They both had kids and although I'm sure they were trained not to get too attached to their cases, you could see it was hard for them. From the way they looked at and spoke to my parents, you could see this wasn't just a job for them. They'd probably had to do this countless times before with other families and it didn't seem to get any easier for them. When we cried, or got angry and demanded answers, they were there to help and I began to realize that the police weren't always the ogres they were made out to be. I really believed that if everybody could see this caring, sensitive side to them and recognize the fact that most of them went into the job wanting to help others, then a better relationship could be formed between the public and the police. My new-found respect for the police didn't go unnoticed, though. I know that a few people in my area were laughing at me and, because I had started to work with them on my campaign and throughout my journey, were even calling me a 'grass', but I didn't care. These were the only people who could get my brother some sort of justice so these were the people my loyalty lay with.

When we got into the Old Bailey, Mandy had some bad news for us. Apparently, all three of the defendants were now turning up in person to give their pleas. I was horrified. I'd only come because I was assured they wouldn't be here and now I'd have to face them. I automatically blamed the liaison officers for misleading us but it really wasn't their fault. It was up to the defendants' lawyers and if they wanted to change their minds at the last minute they could – they didn't care about our feelings, they didn't care about the further impact and shock it would have on my family, they just wanted to do the best for their clients.

I knew I could go home if I wanted to but now I was here it was better to get it over and done with. If my mum and dad could put on a brave face then so could I. Maybe once I'd seen them any power or fear I believed they had over me would be gone. We went up to the canteen and waited for court to commence, all sipping at awful coffee, nobody saying much at all.

At half past ten, half an hour after we were meant to start, the police went down to find out what the delay was. It took a long time but finally they came back and sheepishly said that although two of the defendants were in the building, they had 'lost' the other one. We all looked at each other in horror – what did that mean? Had he escaped? Was he now on the loose laughing at his luck, about to disappear forever? We were assured that wasn't the case at all – quite simply, they didn't know if he was on his way to court, or already in the building, or still sitting in his cell somewhere far away.

I couldn't understand. Surely they had radios and communication systems that would allow them to find out. How could they not know where he was? I began to get so angry and couldn't believe this was happening to my family. It was bad enough that we had to go through all this but to now be told that one of the men accused of killing Ben had disappeared was the last straw.

Finally, after two hours of hanging around and being told that we might have to delay the plea hearing to another day, the police said he had finally arrived and was in the building. Now that everybody was there, the show could get started.

When I was told earlier that morning they would be attending court, I'd built up my courage and was determined to be as brave as my brother had been and look them in the eyes. However, after waiting around for all that time, I'd begun to lose my confidence and wasn't sure I could do it. We all silently filed into the court. My parents and I were downstairs in the actual courtroom with the lawyers, police and the judge. As we took our seats on the hard, uncomfortable bench I glanced up to the public gallery, not expecting to see anybody. To my surprise, there were a couple of our family members there to support us.

We hadn't told anybody about today. I knew the date had been released in the press but we hadn't invited anybody as, first, it was meant to be a small, formal hearing and, secondly, we didn't want crowds of people turning up and causing a scene. Although it was nice to have some support, it amazed me that nothing could be kept quiet and intimate when it came to things like murder.

Scanning across, I saw a couple of girls hanging over the balcony, looking directly at me with stony, nasty glares. I didn't recognize them but I knew instantly they were from the 'other side'. I tried to look away but couldn't help being infuriated. Every time I looked up at my family, there they were giving me dirty looks and trying to intimidate me. I wished then that I had my sister Jade with me. Growing up, I was lucky enough never to have had a fight or even a scuffle. I wasn't one for confrontation, automatically bursting into tears any time anybody started on me, never able to stand up for myself. It was Jade, the sister who was three years younger than me but ten times tougher, who fought my battles. Even though I was meant to protect her, it was Jade who'd been head-butted when a girl tried to pick a fight with me, it was Jade who got punched in the head when a man tried to steal my mobile phone, and it was Jade who would have told these girls where to go.

But she wasn't there and it was time I learned to defend myself. I hadn't been able to defend my brother but I would not let these people get to me and the rest of my family. I didn't want to lower myself to their level but I wouldn't let them think they would win.

Our staring match was broken by the clerk calling, 'All rise.' Everybody stood up as the judge came in and then my heart stopped as, one by one, three men entered the room.

They were dressed in normal men's clothes – jeans, trendy T-shirts and jumpers. They walked with their heads lowered, their eyes looking everywhere but at me and my parents. They smiled up at their friends and were led into the dock. To my absolute horror, I realized that the small wooden area I was sitting next to was the dock they would be standing in. If I reached out my hand, I could have touched the one nearest to me. There was no glass, no barrier, they weren't in handcuffs – they could have jumped over and done anything to us and we in return could have done the same to them.

For someone who hadn't wanted to see them, I couldn't take my eyes off them. There was nothing even remotely remarkable about their appearance. They didn't look like monsters, you couldn't recognize the evil in them; you'd have walked past all of them in the street without a second glance. The only distinguishing feature of any of them was that one was over six feet tall. My brother had been tall but this man was a lot taller and I pictured him, towering over Ben, menacing and dangerous. He was the one closest to me. The one in the middle looked the scariest. He didn't look like someone you would necessarily be frightened of, he didn't look like a big, tough man, but he had a hard, expressionless face and showed not even the slightest bit of remorse. In fact, none of them did. The last one looked about fourteen. I knew he wasn't, of course. I knew he was a fully grown man completely responsible for his actions, but he had such a baby face that I couldn't believe he was potentially a murderer.

Actually, I couldn't believe any of them were. For months I had pictured these awful, terrifying thugs, yet these men looked absolutely normal. They didn't look like they had the power or the strength to end the life of my brother – I was sure I could have taken them all on myself. But they didn't use power or strength. They were cowards and had hidden behind a knife.

I fought the urge to jump on them, to hurt them, to scream at them and demand, 'Why?' I could feel the vibrations of my mum's leg shaking the whole bench, and could almost see the rage emanating from my dad. This wasn't fair. This wasn't fair on any of us.

The rest of the hearing was a blur of legal talk and arguments. Only a couple of things stood out – the first being that when the judge demanded to know why the third defendant had arrived late, his lawyer stated that he'd had a 'horrific' journey, had been stuck in traffic and was very distressed about it all – poor, poor thing.

The second was when one of them applied for bail. My heart stopped – surely there wasn't even a *chance* of bail, not for a charge as serious as murder. His lawyer claimed that since being imprisoned he'd been a model prisoner and had been very well behaved, as if this was a good enough reason to let him go. It didn't matter what he may have done previously, he'd managed to behave himself for the next four months so apparently that meant all was forgiven.

Thankfully, he didn't get bail, but I couldn't believe the way the system worked. I didn't understand how these lawyers could defend people who were being accused of crimes like this. I'm not naive – I know that our society needs these lawyers because sometimes people are innocent and that everyone is entitled to a fair trial, but when you're looking at it from a victim's perspective, when you've lost someone you love at the hands of another, it's hard to see any fairness at all.

Finally, it was time for them to plead. We all held our breath. Everybody else looked almost bored, as if they'd seen this a thousand times before, which they probably had. However, for us it was all new and so important. This was it. This was their chance to redeem themselves.

When asked, the first boy, Braithwaite, looked straight ahead and said firmly, 'Not guilty.' My heart sank. He said it in a surprised voice, as if he had no idea why he was here, being made to answer to everyone like this. The second man, Alleyne, again said, 'Not guilty,' in a voice full of attitude, that let everybody know he thought the court was wasting his time when he clearly had better things to do. The third man, Kika – baby-face – when

Above: Me, aged 8 and Jade aged 6, ecstatic at the arrival of our baby brother Ben

Right: Ben, 17 months old and already fooling around

Below: Happy Families – Me and my siblings Jade, Ben, Georgia, Christopher and Holly

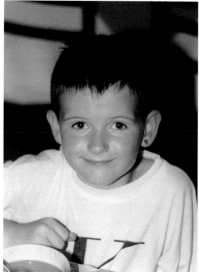

Ben in Cyprus aged 6, the only time he
ever went abroad

Ben, aged 5 and Georgia, aged 2, all
dressed up for Halloween

My favourite possession – a drawing
done for me by Ben when he was
younger

Twins! – Ben showing off
his cheeky grin, aged 14

Me, Jade, Ben and his friend Jack at a
fancy dress party the year before he
died – Ben wanted to go as a kissing
booth but ended up as Mr Muscle

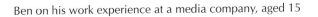

Ben on his work experience at a media company, aged 15

Ben at his beloved
Arsenal's homeground,
aged 15

A beautiful legacy – Ben's
GCSE artwork, a batik print,
earned him an A* grade

His 'K' design – drawn
on every item he owned
and now recognised
nationwide

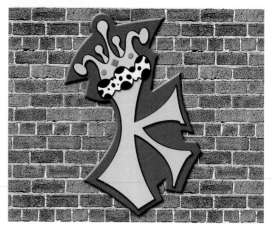

A poignant image that sums up the feelings of our community when we marched for Ben just days after he was murdered

A candelight vigil was held for Ben in the days following his death and the turnout was amazing

Me working with the Sunderland Police as part of my journey to learn more about knife crime

Me and my documentary crew after interviewing Gordon Brown!

One of the hardest parts of my journey was looking at the horrific weapons that have been confiscated from our streets

Me at the school I visited in New York with some of the very young ex-gang members

Me and my family outside the Old Bailey just after the verdict was announced

Justice at last . . .

asked, choked on his words and mumbled so quietly that the clerk had to ask him to repeat his plea. 'Not guilty,' he almost whispered. It was then that I knew for sure. They knew what they'd done that night. They could pretend they were innocent, so could their lawyers, so could we all. We would give them their fair trial but I knew in my heart that they were the reason my brother had died that night. In the delivery of his answer, the third man had given away his fear and their guilt and I prayed that eventually everybody else would see it also.

At the end of the hearing, their lawyers asked that the defendants be allowed to return to the prisons they were currently being held in as they were more comfortable there and had had 'difficulties' at previous ones. I didn't care what these difficulties were, I didn't care how uncomfortable they were – prison life was meant to be hard. I didn't want them to have an easy time. However, the judge agreed and I knew then that we had a long, hard road ahead of us. I'd heard from other victims and families that the justice system sometimes let you down, that it seemed as if the criminals had all the rights and you had none, but I didn't want to believe it. If you are accused of killing somebody, surely your right to be 'comfortable' should be of no concern.

I couldn't understand. I knew the police had been a great help and support to us but I hadn't realized that everything was out of their control now. They had done their best, they had found the evidence, they had caught and charged people and delivered them into the legal system. Their job was done.

We watched the defendants walk out of the dock, smiling again to their people above them. I wanted to scream. I wanted them to look at us before they went and really see what they'd done, but not once did they ever look our way.

The start date for the actual trial was set for 21 April 2009, six months later, and until then, there was nothing more we could do. It seemed unfair that we had to wait that long. By the time the trial came round, Ben would have been gone almost a year, and we may have started to attempt to get our lives back to some normality. I seriously doubted it, as I didn't think we could ever have a 'normal' life again, but by then maybe we all would have tried to go back to work, Georgia would be in the middle of her GCSEs, we'd be attempting to live again. But then we'd be thrown straight back to square one, dragged back to that awful night where we'd have to hear the horrific details of what went on. We'd be unable to work for the weeks the trial took place, unable to concentrate or focus on anything else and, when it was all finally over, we'd have to start all over again. There hardly seemed any point in trying. The only thing that would make it worth it was if we got the verdict we wanted, and that was only a possibility. My brother's justice and our sanity rested in the hands of the courts, a judge and twelve completely random strangers. It seemed to us like we had no hope at all.

Chapter 10

Happy Birthday, Benjamina. Seventeen today. I hope that wherever you are you wake up and have somebody to say this to you. I hope that angels are still allowed to have birthdays because I know how much you love them.

I hope that somebody has given you a lovely present, and made a fuss of you all day but, most importantly, I hope they have brought you a big chocolate cake, for your birthday would not be complete without one.

We wake up crying and we don't stop until this awful day is over. Birthdays are supposed to be days of laughter and happiness, not heartbreak and tears.

You should be here to get your first driving lesson. We should be able to see your face light up as you run out the door and jump into the car, something that you've wanted since you picked up your first toy one.

You used to drive me mad, begging me to teach you to drive. I'm the worst driver in the world – it took me four attempts to pass my test but you still wanted me to teach you. Even though I only had a battered old Nissan Micra, you couldn't wait to get behind the wheel and show everyone what you could do. I don't even think you ever got the chance to sit behind a wheel. I can't believe there are so many things you will now never get to do.

You should be here to receive your presents from us and then spend the day with your friends, going out for pizza as is your tradition. Then maybe we'd all join you and buy you a cherry beer and you'd smile and say, 'One year 'til I'm eighteen now!' One more year and you would have been a man.

There are no presents and no cake and no pizza or cherry beers for you or us. Instead, we go to your grave. It's cold now that it's nearly winter, and I can't believe you will spend your seventeenth birthday here.

People have been up and left cards and balloons and I've bought you a birthday card, with a badge that says, 'The Best Bro in the World'. In my card, I write as if you're still here. I write as I've written every birthday card for you for the past seventeen years. I say the words out loud as I'm writing too in case you don't get to read it, but can hear me when I speak to you.

I nearly bought you a present too. Normally, you ask for money and buy the things you've wanted all year, spending it all in an hour then finding a hundred more things you wanted the next day. I can't give you money but I rack my brains trying to think of something I can leave with you, something you'll still get to enjoy.

Finally, I decide to name a star after you. There is a constellation whose name means 'King' and I'll put your star in there. On your birthday every year, I'll leave something of you in this world. I'll name a star, adopt a monkey, grow a tree and call them all Ben. It's not as good as computer games or new trainers, I know, but it will have to do.

We sit by your grave and cry and whisper, 'Happy Birthday', and leave our cards and flowers among the rest. We kiss the wooden cross – it's too early for you to have a headstone, your ground needs to settle yet – and we go.

It's colder in our house than it was in the cemetery. We want to shake ourselves out of the depression and gloom and celebrate your birthday for you, as you'd have wanted to. We try our hardest to smile and make your day special but we just can't do it. Instead we all go to our separate beds and fall asleep crying.

Never mind, there's always next year. Not for you, no more next year for you, my angel, but for us. I have a feeling it's only going to get harder.

After the setback of the plea hearing and Ben's birthday, I was ready to get working on the campaign again. I *needed* to get working again. Every time I stopped and let myself think about what had happened, I would get swept away in a wave of pain and depression that was hard to escape. I knew that delaying my grief would probably have bad consequences for me but, at the moment, it was the only way I could deal with it.

I really felt like I'd got somewhere, not only in London,

but across the country. I'd even been up to Sunderland in the Northeast and shadowed police there to see what they were doing about the problem.

They had put some great ideas in practice. In most secondary schools, there was a local police team always on site, there to provide safety and advice. This meant they got to know most of the kids and began to form some kind of relationship with them. Therefore, if they ever caught them misbehaving on the street, it was easier to tell them to stop and have some respect shown back because the respect had been built and was mutual.

They also had an ASBO-type scheme where, if kids were caught drinking in the park or behaving in a threatening or rowdy way, they were issued with a 'warning'. This warning was in the form of a computerized slip, very much like a parking ticket, which went straight onto the system and saved a great deal of paperwork and time. Once the kid had received three warnings, they were 'out' and were given a form of ASBO. This ASBO included a curfew, the potential loss of their family home, fines, etc. It made parents sit up and take notice of their children's behaviour and whereabouts, as none of them wanted to lose their home.

While I was working with them, they were also road-testing metal-detecting arches in clubs and pubs to deter people from bringing weapons in and were having some degree of success. They were using the new metal-detecting wands to search people and I witnessed them dealing with youngsters and asking to search them. Many were more open to it because they felt it wasn't as intrusive as being searched physically.

Sunderland didn't have the same level of problems with gangs as we did in London and other major cities but they had their fair share of knife crime and were trying their best to combat it. Again, I got the impression that the police were trying their best but were held back by low funding and limited powers.

I decided that I needed to continue my research and look at a city that did have the same levels of problems as we did, yet had managed to turn it around. We had already made some good changes in Britain but I still felt there was a lot more to do – I was still looking for that big national scheme or plan that we could all be a part of and get behind.

I remembered my brother's letter to Gordon Brown, and how he'd mentioned New York. He'd said that it was once the most dangerous city in the world and yet they had reduced their crime rate over the past few years, and it was then that I knew where the next step of my journey was.

In the past, New York has been notorious for violent crime, yet in the last twelve years, their crime rate has dropped by 75 per cent, and in 2005, their murder rate was the lowest it had been since 1963.

They did this by introducing more police officers onto the streets and by adopting the 'broken windows' policy. Before

I went to New York, I attended a Labour Party conference on knife crime and met Chief Bill Bratton, formerly the head of the New York Police Department and now chief of the LAPD. He made a speech at the beginning of the conference explaining what he and his officers had done to help reduce crime and got the loudest cheer of all. He spoke from the heart and said that people had to stop blaming it on the economy, on poverty, on the weather and start taking responsibility.

He then explained the concept of the 'broken windows' policy to me. He told me to imagine a building with a few broken windows. If the windows aren't repaired, the tendency is for vandals to come along and break a few more windows. Eventually, they'll break into the building and, if it's left unoccupied, will perhaps become squatters, or commit arson, or turn it into a drug den.

Or consider a pavement. Some people throw litter. If that isn't picked up, then more people throw litter. Eventually people start leaving bags of rubbish everywhere, they stop caring about their neighbourhood, stop wanting to take care of it and small crimes such as car theft and burglary arise.

He was basically saying that if you take care of the smaller crimes, it will potentially stop the chain leading to bigger crimes. Of course, this wouldn't stop crime altogether but it could have an effect on the root causes.

In New York, they put this policy into practice by deciding to clean up the subway system. They cleaned all the graffiti off the walls, they put money into the transport system and then they started a zero-tolerance initiative with fare dodgers. By stopping the fare dodgers, they found that some offenders were illegal immigrants, some were carrying weapons or drugs, some were drunk and disorderly. Slowly, the 'cleaning' began to spread from the subway to the streets and the crime rate fell.

There are criticisms of this plan. It could be said that by focusing on the smaller crimes, more serious crimes are being ignored, and also that it criminalizes the poor, focusing on street crimes and excluding white-collar offences like fraud and embezzlement.

Despite this, you couldn't argue that New York wasn't trying, and they'd definitely had some success in turning their situation around.

Chief Bratton told me I should go out there and look at some of the great social schemes they had set up, so in November 2008, I found myself on a plane to New York, with my documentary crew behind me.

When I landed in New York, I had a few hours' sleep to get over the jet-lag before it was time for the hard work to start.

The first programme I was researching in America was called Council For Unity. I'd never heard of it before but it turned out it was very well known and popular, not only in New York, where it originated, but nationally and overseas too.

Council For Unity was created in 1975 in Brooklyn by

Bob DeSena, an English teacher. He'd had enough of the violence and gang warfare that ruled many of the schools in Brooklyn and so he recruited six renowned gang leaders and asked them to join him and help end the vicious cycle.

This had never been attempted before. Gang members – especially leaders – didn't come together for anything except to hurt or kill each other. When I arrived in New York, Bob DeSena was the first person I met and he was my tour guide for the first few days. He looked like any ordinary man but his charisma and passion for what he was doing shone out and it was easy to see why he had been so successful. Although he came across as extremely confident, he told me of his fear of putting all those gang members in one room for the first time, and the worry of not knowing whether they'd agreed to meet simply to have an opportunity to get at each other or because they genuinely wanted to help.

At first there was no backing down from anybody, but eventually they began to talk about what their problems were and soon realized that they didn't even know why they hated each other or had been fighting for so long.

This non-violent way of solving things was a revelation and Bob built on that by creating a model for all schools. This model was grounded in what he called 'FUSE', standing for Family, Unity, Self-esteem and Empowerment. It basically meant that all members of the Council would follow these principles and treat each other with respect and warmth, bring together communities and schools to create a safe and tolerant environment, allow themselves and others to develop skills and talents to provide motivation and, most importantly, allow the youth to run the programmes. Bob believed that responsibility cannot be taught; it must be experienced.

In the simplest terms, in schools where people were being bullied and forced to enter gangs and live a life they'd never wanted, Bob provided a different 'family' to join – one that didn't coerce you to commit crime but encouraged you to concentrate on your talents. Most kids were scared that if they didn't join a gang they'd have nowhere else to turn, but Council For Unity provided them with a different option and a form of protection.

The programme was made rewarding and popular by the fact it was introduced as an actual academic class kids could take and get graded on. Many kids joined thinking it would be an easy A-grade but once they got there and got involved, they found it hard not to get swept up in the transformations.

By the time I discovered Council For Unity, it was touching the lives of over 100,000 kids annually and was in over forty schools and ninety-six chapters in New York State. I wanted to see the Council in action for myself because, though it sounded like a great idea, I couldn't understand how they managed to get these kids to sit down and listen in the first place.

I was told that the gang problem is one of the single

greatest issues the New York educational system is facing today. Although it used to be older teenagers getting involved, now children as young as nine or ten years old were being recruited into gangs, many of them picked up in the school environment. Kids were joining to become more popular, because they were scared, for protection – whatever the reason, the demand had become so high that most schools were calling on Bob to do gang-prevention classes and try to help in some way.

The school I visited was called Sheepshead Bay High School. When I walked through the school entrance, I stopped in shock. At every door were big metal arches and by every arch were at least two security guards or police officers. I'd been told that this school had had a massive problem with violent crime but I couldn't believe it was necessary to have this amount of security. Everywhere I looked kids were having their bags or pockets searched and, although it was time-consuming, no one seemed to have a problem with it. As one kid told me later, 'I'd rather have my bag searched than be stabbed or shot.'

I saw very few white kids at the school. Afro-American, Hispanic and Asian – children of different cultures walked everywhere and I now knew why racism played such a big part in gang creation here, as each ethnic group seemed to keep totally to itself. In London, most people are extremely tolerant of other races and, even though that was probably true of other areas in New York, in this environment and with this generation, there seemed to be problems.

However, if anybody was an outsider it was me. As I walked along the corridors I was stared at brazenly and dirty looks and sniggers were aimed at me. These kids didn't know who I was and they didn't care. I was actually scared of twelve-year-old children, but I defy anybody not to feel as I did if placed in that environment and so out of your comfort zone.

One lady who'd accompanied us while doing her own research was wearing a fur coat, but this was taken off her immediately when she entered the building to avoid 'temptation'.

After meeting the head teacher, we were taken to the first Council For Unity class that day, where I would observe a meeting of the Council. We took our places at the small, battered desks, the camera crew started filming and we waited silently as the kids filed in.

The kids that walked in that door looked scarier than any I had ever seen. Ripped clothes, big hair, pierced body parts – there seemed to be no sense of uniform or discipline. They were chewing gum, talking loudly, kicking chairs – not paying one bit of attention to the English people in the corner. Finally, the teacher stood up and announced that Council was in session. He told the kids to ignore the cameras and just do what they normally did. Nothing happened and I began to think this could be a waste of time. These kids clearly weren't going to open up to outsiders and why should they? They had created their own little world and didn't want anybody invading it.

Then, one by one, they came out of their shell. With prompting from the teacher, they began to talk about why they had joined Council and what it had done for them. Many of them had been new kids who couldn't fit in and didn't know where to turn, only knowing they didn't want to become a gang member. Many had been 'jumped' or beaten severely, either as an initiation ritual or simply for fun. The discussion about initiations turned my stomach and almost made me walk out. An initiation was when you had to perform a task to prove yourself to the gang. The task was often in the form of a crime, and while before it may have been robbery or mugging, more recently the initiations had turned more and more violent, with gang leaders demanding that 'pledges' – new members – hurt and sometimes kill people to show their loyalty. One of the most notorious initiation rituals was the 'Buck 150'. This involved cutting somebody with a knife so badly that they needed 150 stitches to sew them up. I heard that only the day before I'd landed in New York, over fifty women had had this happen to them as part of some awful Halloween ritual. It was sickening.

Some of the kids had older siblings who were involved in gang life who expected the younger ones to follow their example, and some were gang leaders themselves – kids who at the age of only fifteen had done unspeakable things to other people.

I felt sick as I heard what some of these kids had got up to. Many of the boys carried weapons on a daily basis and weren't afraid to use them – some had stabbed and others had been stabbed and they proudly lifted up shirts and trouser legs to show me their scars. Even the girls would carry knives. The fashionable choice was a 'lipstick' knife – a knife disguised as a make-up item that flicked open a blade. Many girls wore razor blades in their hair in case boys tried to touch them or girls tried to fight them. Gun crime was also a problem, with many kids carrying them or being wounded by them.

After a while the kids let me ask them a few questions. I couldn't believe the life these kids were living at such a young age and couldn't understand how they had got caught up in this.

I wasn't impressed by their answer that they'd had no other choice or they were made to, as surely if they'd really wanted to live a different life they could have? I was getting angry that these young people may have done to others what had been done to my brother and didn't even seem that sorry for it.

However, the more I listened, the more I realized it was unfair for me to judge. It was easy to say I'd have acted differently, that I wouldn't have been forced into this life if it was me, but I'd never been put in that position. And these were the kids who were trying to change. Yes, they had carried weapons, had maybe even used them – although not to the extent of murder (or not that they were admitting!) – but they wanted to end it before it went too far and they killed another person or were killed themselves.

I listened to how they had changed since joining Council. One girl whose temper was so bad she used to get into fights daily was now a changed person. One kid who was being badly bullied now had more confidence and a 'family' to look after him. Their schoolwork was better, their grades were higher – most of them were graduating that year and going on to college.

The biggest change was in the boy who led the meeting. He had been a former gang member high up the chain of command. He spoke of hurting other people and not really knowing why he did it until one day he decided enough was enough. It was hard to leave the gang and he was constantly looking over his shoulder and fearing for his life but he'd made his decision. He turned his life around and started trying to get others involved in Council, to get others to change their lives as well.

This talk of life-changing shocked me. These kids were between the ages of thirteen and sixteen, they should have been just beginning their lives, but instead they had to start over? It seemed a lot to handle. Although I couldn't justify or forgive them for picking up weapons, I could at least begin to understand their reasons for doing so and had to admire them for trying to stop.

The amazing thing about Council was that it was completely run by the kids. There was a teacher there to supervise but it was chaired and led by the kids and all the decisions were made by them. This was the reason it worked. Kids didn't want to be dictated to or lectured, they wanted to figure out the problems themselves, which is why they often turned to violence, because for some it was the only way they knew of solving things on their own. However, by giving them a different environment and allowing them to make their own choices, it seemed they were realizing they'd been doing it wrong and were trying to make amends.

They made moral decisions – things like allowing a gay boy into their Council. Even though some members were originally against it, others reminded them of what Council was about and how there should be no discrimination. The boy was desperate to be a part of Council as he'd had a tough time since joining the school and was devastated when he thought they wouldn't allow him to participate. However, those who were against it knew how wrong it would be to veto him and not only did they let him in, they protected him from any further bullying and changed his life dramatically.

I could see that Council For Unity was changing the lives of many kids. This was just one class in one school but it was already making a difference. As this programme was happening all over New York, it must have been having a great impact.

I didn't know if there were any schemes like this in Britain but I knew there should be. For all those that argued about rehabilitation and prevention, this was the perfect thing. It still didn't excuse some of the things these kids had done but the programme was helping them not to hurt anybody else, and kids that had never hurt anyone were deterred early on from doing so.

One of the girls I'd spoken to struck a particular chord in me – although she hadn't hurt anyone yet, I could see she had fire in her eyes and anger in her face. I knew she hadn't had an easy life but she had joined Council in the hope it would help her before she ever let her demons loose. I gave her a hug before I went – carefully watching out for razor blades in her hair – and walked back out through the metal detectors. This would be a hard place to grow up in, to be educated in, but I knew the kids were a thousand times happier and safer now than they had been a few years ago, thanks to the strict security measures applied and, of course, Council For Unity.

Once it had become successful in schools, Council then branched out to entire communities – businesses, youth organizations, law enforcement. Anywhere there was racism or violence, if they were invited in, they would respond.

For me, the biggest surprise was that it was introduced into prisons. Bob had taken it into jails – where all that existed was violence and racism and gang warfare. At first it had been immediately dismissed but he had persevered and, just like when he originally started out, had per-suaded certain gang leaders who were in prison to come on board and influence the rest.

I was asked to visit Suffolk County Jail – a holding place for those who were awaiting bail hearings or sentencing.

It was basically a prison for men aged sixteen and upwards, men who'd committed a variety of crimes ranging from robbery to murder.

I wasn't really sure what I was going to be doing there, apart from interviewing some of the prison guards and seeing Council in action. I was escorted through security and immediately led into a room where over thirty men in green jumpsuits turned and looked at me.

I'd never been so scared in my life. They looked at me like I was an alien, and to them I suppose I was. A small white girl with a camera crew behind her, standing there with a petrified expression on her face. Once again, there were very few white men here, many were black or Hispanic, many of them about my age, staring at me and waiting for me to talk.

But I wasn't there to talk, I was there to observe. There was no way I was going to talk to these dangerous, frightening men and so I shuffled to a seat at the back of the room and waited for the meeting to begin.

The prison guard got up to start the meeting and then introduced me and the crew to the prisoners. She started to explain why we were there but then, to my horror, turned to me and said, 'Actually, Brooke, why don't you come up and talk to them and explain what you're doing?'

I literally couldn't move. I couldn't get up there and talk to those men. For a start, I was shaking with fear and, secondly, there was no way they were going to listen to me. These were some of the most hardened criminals – they would have no time for a young girl and her sob story.

However, there was no getting out of it and so I slowly walked up the aisle to the front of the room, all eyes on me, my legs nearly giving way with every step.

I couldn't believe how different my life now was. A few months ago I'd been performing a play in a theatre in Hackney and now I was speaking to an audience of prisoners in New York.

I didn't have a clue how to relate to them and decided it wasn't even worth trying to play it cool or act tough – I was simply going to tell them the truth.

I told them about my brother's murder and how it had led me here and that quite simply all I wanted was to find a way to stop it. I explained that as most of them were here for committing serious crimes, maybe they could give me some insight as to why this went on and also settle the argument as to whether jail was tough enough and the best solution or whether they thought there was a better way.

To my surprise, as I was talking, they all listened intently and some even nodded along with my points. I thought they'd assume I was there to preach and lecture them on what they'd done, and maybe make them feel bad if they too had committed violent crimes, but once they saw that all I was looking for was help, they began to warm to me. As I finished my introduction and walked away, they all started to clap and it made me smile. I didn't understand why it felt so good to be admired by a group of convicts but, for some reason, it did.

The Council For Unity programme in jail was very similar to the ones in the schools. They also used non-violent methods to solve problems and really highlighted talking and discussing things, rather than acting on them. It was amazing to see men who I was told were some of the most notorious gang members in New York shake hands and sit down and talk to each other. Again, Bob was apprehensive about introducing this programme in prisons, and especially to gang members, because he thought people would use it to spy on rival gangs or, worse, attack them. However, it seemed to work. Gang members stopped becoming rivals and became friends. They didn't call each other by their nicknames or identify each other by their 'colours' or their Blood or Crip tags, they learned each other's first names and also learned respect.

One of the things Bob based the programme on was the concept of 'Dragon Slaying'. This was basically a fairy story about a prince who had to slay a dragon to save his village and all new members would learn this story when they first joined. Meetings would then be based around this story and the themes it brought up, with many members 'slaying' their own dragons and talking about why they had done the things they had, talking about their violent pasts and facing their demons.

At first it sounded too childlike and I couldn't see how

talking about a fairy tale would help – surely these tough men would laugh at that idea?

But they didn't. They really believed in it and used the morals and values they learned to try and apply them to their own lives. Just like the kids in the schools, they were tired of the path they were on and wanted to make a change, though for some of them it seemed too late, especially when they were looking at a lifetime in jail.

They didn't take that attitude, though. It didn't matter if they were in jail or on the streets, they wanted a better life for themselves and Council helped them achieve that. By joining, they were allowed access to educational classes and schemes they wouldn't have otherwise had, and many of them gained degrees or diplomas in subjects they enjoyed.

The best part of being a Council member was that it allowed them to help others. Some men came into prison looking for a fight because they expected that was how life was, but Council members would talk to them and advise them to join, therefore reducing violence and forming more trust and respect in the prisons.

I know it may not sound like that big a deal, especially when these people had already committed crimes and were locked away for a long time, but you have to witness it to really appreciate the impact.

For me, it brought up many awful conflicts. If I liked this programme so much and believed it would work, would I want the people who'd done this to my brother to participate? Would I want them to study subjects they enjoyed and gain qualifications my brother never could? Would I be able to sit and smile and congratulate them on their changes like I had these prisoners? The thought made me feel sick. No, I couldn't. It might be hypocritical and it might be pig-headed, but I could never sit and applaud them for something they had done, no matter how good it was. I could, however, admit that I would rather them be taking part in a programme like this behind bars, a programme that might reform them even a little bit, even though the change would come too late for Ben. I would rather this than have them continuing along the same path, murdering other people's sons and other people's brothers.

Chapter 11

Your biggest dream was to travel the world, especially to America. It was all you spoke about: how when you were eighteen you would go to college in America and live there for a few years. We would smile indulgently but knew there was no way we would ever let you go that far, we would miss you too much.

If you couldn't go to America, you still wanted to go on holiday. Every year you begged us to go away as a family, and every year we couldn't – Mummy hated flying, there was never enough money, never enough time. We always said, maybe next year.

It turned out there never was a next year and so we never got to go on holiday together as a family. I never got to see you get excited on a plane, splash around in a pool, lie happily in the sun. The only time you ever went on a plane was when you were three and you went on holiday with our Nan. I look at pictures of you building sandcastles and eating ice cream and wish I had real memories instead.

You'll never get to travel the world now, never see any other country, never be able to go to America, and so we decide to go there for you. Even Mummy gets on that plane and although she's shaking with fear the whole time, she's doing it for you. I know you must be so proud of her.

My favourite bit is when we are at the highest point in the clouds because I feel it's the closest I've been to you since you left. Maybe you're floating around outside, maybe even within reach, and for the whole flight, I search every cloud for your face.

In New York, we try and do everything for you. We go sightseeing in the pouring rain, we eat Hershey chocolate bars and Oreos, your favourites. We walk past all the designer clothes in silence, sad in the knowledge that if you were here you'd be in your element, emptying Mummy's purse in minutes.

We put your picture on our hotel windowsill so you can look out at the view and wherever we go, we leave your badge as a mark. In fact, many people are doing this – so far you've been to Spain, Thailand, Japan, Mexico – everybody takes a badge and leaves it in the places they have visited, so at least you're travelling the world in some way.

I stare across at the Statue of Liberty and picture you standing beside me, laughing and saying, 'It's not that big.' I picture you playing jokes on the tourists like you do at home, making me cry with laughter, and I'm so upset that I'll never get to do these things with you again. That I'll never get to have fun with you again.

But it doesn't matter, as I'm not here for fun. I'm here to work. You've sent me here for a reason, to find a solution, and I won't stop until I do.

Although I went to New York with my documentary crew for research, I decided to take my mum and sister with me too for a couple of days to give them a break. It was halfway through my trip to New York that I believed I'd finally found the answer I was looking for: the programme that would help solve our problem, the scheme that would keep everybody happy – one that involved extreme discipline but also invaluable treatment and rehabilitation.

On day four I travelled to Buffalo, New York, to visit Lakeview boot camp. The term 'boot camp' may sound like a light-hearted pseudo-military regime but this was anything but. The official name for this programme was 'Shock'.

Lakeview is a correctional facility that houses over a thousand inmates, both male and female. It takes in offenders who are under the age of forty, serving their first prison term and eligible for parole in less than three years. It also has a strict policy of not accepting anybody who's committed a violent or sexual offence, or has taken part in large-scale drug trafficking.

Potential inmates are screened intently for their suitability for Shock and must meet the above criteria, as well as strict physical and mental health checks. Once they are deemed suitable, they have a big decision to make.

If they decide to go ahead with Shock, they will spend

six months in an intense military-themed programme, with all movements controlled by staff, all attitudes and opinions left at the door, and the knowledge that they're in for a lot of hard work and self-discovering.

The 'golden carrot' reward for signing up is that if they manage to complete the programme to everybody's satisfaction, they'll be eligible for parole after six months and won't have to serve the rest of their sentence. If they decide it's too much for them, or if they do not fully comply with the rules, they will immediately be sent back to a general prison and made to serve their entire sentence.

At first, I didn't think this sounded fair. If they'd committed a crime and been sentenced for it, why should they only serve a small part of that sentence? Obviously everybody was going to sign up for this scheme if it was six months of playing at being in the army and then freedom.

Shock, though, is anything but playing. On the first day of my visit, I was woken up at 4 a.m. and told to get a move on or I'd miss the beginning of the day. Still half-asleep, I walked down to the outside campus and saw a sight that woke me up immediately.

There were hundreds of inmates, all dressed in their uniforms, in 'platoons' of around fifty people each. They were lined up exactly so, with not one person an inch out of place. The yard was completely silent – despite the many people and despite it being outside, you could hear a pin drop.

Suddenly a deafening yell came from somewhere in the

middle and through the crowds I saw one solitary drill instructor standing on a platform. He began calling out chants, which were answered back word-for-word perfect. It sounded like songs that would be sung at an American football game, but they all had their own particular rhythm and I soon saw that the point of them was to instil discipline, morale and a beat for the exercises they began doing.

For half an hour they did a workout that would put even the biggest gym freak to shame. Many of them struggled, some were obviously overweight, some simply hated being there, but there was not one complaint, they all just got on with it.

What shocked me was that there were hundreds of them and only one member of staff – if they'd wanted to, they could easily have overpowered him but they didn't. They were only going to get out of here if they did it the hard way.

After the exercises they filed off and I assumed they were going for their breakfast. When I asked, however, I was told that that wasn't the case – they were now going off for their daily five-mile run.

Physical training is a very important part of the Shock programme. It instils discipline, is used to make the inmates work out their anger and frustrations and, quite simply, it's there to get them in better shape both mentally and physically. One boy who went there lost an amazing nine stone in the six months he was an inmate. While it looked incredibly harsh and punishing, it was also there for a better reason than that. Yes, push-ups were given out when somebody did something wrong or showed attitude, but the discipline was ultimately there to help these people.

It was hard watching the women do exactly the same exercises as the men. Some of them were tiny but there was no slacking off here, no allowances made – everybody had to complete the programme properly.

Physical training only makes up 25 per cent of the daily Shock regime. Although the inmates are on their feet all day and aren't allowed to rest from the moment they wake up until they go back to bed, not even for one second, there are many, many other aspects to this programme.

The rest of the day is devoted to academic and vocational study, community-service work, drug and alcohol rehabilitation and counselling. I was intrigued that even if you didn't have a problem with substances and had never touched one in your life, you still had to go through this treatment. The underlying reason was that everybody here was addicted to something – whether it be crime, substance, self-harm – they all had to face their demons.

I wandered through classrooms watching inmates studying intently – every subject under the sun. Many walk out of Shock with the equivalent of a high school diploma in under six months and this can be life-changing. The opportunity to study and receive a proper education makes many of the inmates want a better life and motivates them to change.

Although the programme was doing amazing things, it was extremely gruelling. All inmates, men and women, have their heads shaved to an inch on entering the building. While I was there, I saw new inmates who were due to have this happen the next day, girls with hair down to their bottoms who couldn't stop crying at what they would lose.

There's no make-up, no luxury or personal items. They're given two uniforms when they arrive, one for physical training and one for school, and that's all they possess.

They have five minutes to eat every meal, five minutes to get washed, five minutes to do anything. If they misbehave or step out of line, they have to wear a sash that identifies them as a troublemaker and are made to carry all their belongings around with them wherever they go, because the next time they make a mistake they'll be kicked out and sent back to 'real' prison.

Their 'personal' space is a tiny single bed and a minute locker – not much but it's all they need. When they enter into their platoon, they're assigned a number and this is what they'll be known as for the next six months.

They are stripped of everything – their identities, their manners and attitudes, their personalities. It may sound horrific but for many of the inmates it's all they want – the chance to start again and retrain themselves as people, to become somebody different.

I spoke to the instructors and they likened the inmates to boxers who were training for the big fight. As tough as Shock is, the real struggle starts when they're back out in the real world, facing those addictions and demons again, and so the staff try to prepare them for that as best they can.

There were mottos and slogans everywhere I looked – 'Who Dares Wins' and 'You can do it!' It's not all doom and gloom. The instructors are tough but they have to be, and they also look to instil morale at every moment. When inmates want to give up or start to slide weeks before their parole date, they'll fight to make them realize the changes they've made.

Shock was the hardest, toughest regime I'd ever witnessed but it was brilliant. Everybody in there had the utmost respect – they addressed every adult as 'Sir' or 'Ma'am', myself included. It was so strange to have people older than me calling me this and I wanted to tell them to call me Brooke, but they didn't do it out of necessity or because they had to be humbled or humiliated, they did it to show respect.

The differences between those inmates just walking in and those about to leave were astounding. The old inmates stood up straight, they looked you in the eye, they were confident and excited about their future. There was no resentment or hatred about what they'd been through – in fact, they couldn't thank the staff enough for giving them this opportunity.

Why Ben?

I first began researching boot camps because in the early days after my brother's murder, a lot of people were throwing National Service around as a solution. If these kids wanted to pick up a weapon and fight, let them do it for a real reason, let them protect their country. When they got there and saw how tough it really was, and faced the discipline of the army, they wouldn't be such big men then.

I agreed with this. I thought it was a great idea. Why should we send our innocent, well-behaved boys all over the world to die when there were kids who *wanted* to fight? Who wanted to risk their lives every day?

However, it wasn't as easy as that. For a start, our soldiers were having a hard enough time keeping themselves safe without having a bunch of new recruits with attitude who refused to listen and put everyone in danger. Also, to force people into doing something wouldn't help ultimately. It would be some kind of punishment but they wouldn't learn anything, no good would come of it – they would simply rebel and come back twice as angry and dangerous.

I started thinking about having a programme that was similar to the Army. Something that gave people that sort of discipline and order in a controlled setting. To be honest, I hadn't started thinking about rehabilitation yet. I was still of the opinion that criminals should be punished and punished properly – none of this lounging around in prison playing computer games. I wanted them to find it hard.

I decided to go to a boot camp myself, to see what it was all about. I felt I couldn't talk about them as a solution if I had no idea what went on in one.

Just before I went to New York, I spent a week in Devon at the New You Boot Camp and allowed the documentary crew to film me for one day to show how I coped. It was one of the toughest times of my life. It was very similar to Shock in terms of the physical training, but compared to Shock, my boot camp was like a spa. Granted, it was aimed at weight loss and well-being rather than correctional purposes, but it was the only thing I could find in England resembling a military boot camp and I was determined to do my research properly.

At the end of the week I was exhausted and, even after such a short time, I could notice changes in me. Since Ben had been killed, I'd stopped caring about myself and my health, I cried constantly, I felt weak and as if I was only half-living. The boot camp instantly made me stronger. On the first day I could hardly run for two minutes, but by the end I was running up hills for a solid twenty minutes and it gave me such a sense of personal achievement and strength. I actually hated every minute of it but now, when I look back, I appreciate how grateful I am for the experience. It made me stronger mentally too. I didn't cry so easily, I didn't want to just give up, I wanted to keep on running.

It's these mental changes that Shock also brings about. Inmates come in with no sense of self-worth, no self-esteem, many hating themselves and not even wanting to live, which is why they committed crime. They didn't care about the consequences. However, when they've completed the programme, they leave completely changed, determined not to waste another day of their lives.

Again I started to be swayed by the rehabilitation angle some people had been talking about. Had I been wrong all along? I gave this a lot of thought and soon realized that the reason I was so behind the Shock programme was because the people in there had never violently hurt another person. They may have stolen some items or handled some drugs, but they'd never picked up a weapon, never used it on another person, never ripped somebody's life apart.

I'd always maintained that it was much better to help people who'd committed 'minor' crimes rather than send them straight to prison and if it wasn't for Shock, many of these kids would have ended up in proper prison for the rest of their lives.

I didn't mind that these kids would be let off their sentence early – it was worth it to know that the majority of them would never be back in prison again, they would never ruin someone else's life or their own.

I wondered if a programme like this could seriously work in England and honestly couldn't see why it wouldn't. I even believed that it should be used for those who'd committed serious crimes (though with no early release for them). This scheme combined every aspect that people had been arguing about for years – it had the discipline, it had the punishment and the toughness, but it also had rehabilitation, treatment and education. You couldn't argue with the results.

There had to be a catch, a reason it would never work in Britain. When I asked the governor of Lakeview for the costs and efforts involved, he told me that the cost of putting an inmate through Shock is seven pence more per day than keeping them in prison. That's without the money saved by them only being there for six months instead of three years or longer. He also said that it would take a matter of months to set up – it would require a lot of effort but it would be worth it in the end.

He then said something that made my jaw drop. He told me that a few years ago, our then Home Secretary Jack Straw (now Secretary of State for Justice), had come over to visit Lakeview and had absolutely loved the idea. He'd supported it wholeheartedly and said that he would take the idea back to Britain to discuss. Of course, nothing had ever happened. I was so angry. Had a scheme like this been set up years ago, kids might not have become the disrespectful angry people they were, lives might not have been lost, my brother might have still been here – all for a mere seven pence extra a day.

I'm not naive enough to think that Shock would solve everything. I'm sure that not every kid comes out of there and never commits an offence again, but the majority of them don't. This is proven. It's also helped by the fact that when they come out they are under strict parole rules. They must be in their house from seven at night until seven in the morning for the next three years. They're not allowed to touch a drop of alcohol or take drugs and are screened every week to check. Even the smallest violation sends them straight back to jail and these tough measures ensure that these kids stay clean. Many of them haven't even committed that big a crime. One girl was arrested at the age of seventeen and sentenced to four years for carrying a 'dime bag' of marijuana, the smallest amount you can have. It's this strictness that could explain why the crime rate in New York has dropped. Added to that, when they come out of Shock, they're helped to find permanent work or education – in fact, if you come out on a Friday, you start the following Monday. They're not allowed any time or reason to go back to their old lives, to follow the old patterns. Once they have served their sentence and received their punishment, they are helped as much as possible.

I was sure this was what I'd been looking for, what our country needed. I couldn't see any problems with it, any flaws. If anyone argued that it was too harsh or too soft, I begged them to go over and experience the programme for themselves. If we had a scheme like this set in place, it might stop so many kids in their criminal tracks – it might save so many others.

I couldn't stop thinking about it. I finished my trip to New York and, on the plane home, tried to think of a way to tell people about it, to try to get someone to at least think about putting it in place.

Again, the only way I could think to let the country know was to tell my story to the media. I could write a letter to the government, but would they even reply?

As soon as I got home, I did an article for *Reveal* magazine and described what I'd experienced and what I wanted to do now. I spoke angrily about how Jack Straw had seen the boot camp years before and had ignored its potential, and declared that I wanted to deliver this idea to the government and Gordon Brown myself and defy him to give me one good reason why it wouldn't work. I said that I believed they were too busy concentrating on other issues and ignoring the one that was becoming a terrible problem.

I was really scared of speaking out against the government. I had made a big point so far of not entirely blaming any one person or system. It wasn't all the police's fault, it wasn't the schools', it wasn't even just the government's – everybody had to take responsibility.

However, now I knew that this scheme had been brought to their attention a long time ago, I was furious and wasn't going to keep quiet any more. I said my piece and named the people I thought had done wrong and waited for some kind of consequence or comeback.

I didn't ever think I would get anywhere. I was sure that nobody in the government read *Reveal* magazine and thought maybe I should have done it in the *Financial Times*,

———

but I'd also wanted to show the real people, the people who'd supported me the whole way, what I'd learned, to reassure them that I really was trying, I wasn't just pretending.

For the next few days I worried I would get into trouble – from whom I didn't know, but I was sure you couldn't bad-mouth the Prime Minister and get away with it.

A week later, I received a letter from our Prime Minister, Mr Gordon Brown, himself.

Dear Brooke,

I wanted to mention that I have seen the article you wrote for Reveal *magazine about your recent trip to New York. You said that you had learned a great deal about the problem of knife crime and wanted to present me with further proposals to tackle it. I would be very keen to meet you, particularly to listen to your ideas and get your views on some of the action we are planning to take. I will ask my office to contact you to arrange that.*

As you rightly say, whatever other difficulties we are having to deal with as a country, we cannot afford to let the problems of knife crime and gang culture go unchecked, otherwise more young people will be trapped in a cycle of senseless violence and more innocent lives will be lost.

I know that for you and your family, the pain of losing Ben will never go away or get any easier, but the work you are doing to try and prevent other families going through

———

———

that same suffering is truly inspirational, and a great tribute to your brother's memory. I hope that the Government can help you in that cause, and I look forward to meeting you to that end.

Best Wishes

Gordon Brown

I had finally done it. This was my chance.

———

Chapter 12

*You were never fazed when I became some sort of a 'celebrity'.
You never took advantage of it, or swanned around boasting that
I was your sister. If anything, you were highly embarrassed,
especially when I chose to do photoshoots for lads' magazines
such as FHM or Nuts. Lounging around in a bikini, I'd feel
glamorous and sexy but I never gave a thought to my little
brother and the fact that every one of his mates would pick up
these magazines and leer over them.*

*I remember coming home one day and Mummy telling me
you'd been teased over me being in a magazine. You'd almost got
into a fight trying to protect my honour, even though I'd sacri-
ficed that myself. I went up to say sorry but as always you
shrugged and said it didn't matter, and told me to do whatever
I wanted.*

*I'd take you to premieres when you were younger and you'd
be more excited at the chocolate fountains and goody bags than
by any famous people who might have been there. You simply*

didn't care. I'd get you autographs of people I thought you'd find cool, and you'd say thanks and stick them away in a box. It really didn't mean anything to you – you were so proud of me, I know that, but I was still just your big sister, no more.

The one time I completely bowled you over and impressed you was, like the Prada shoes, a fake. I was sitting at a bar and a very big, muscular man began to chat me up. After a while, he told me he was a wrestler and – only out of politeness, because I had no idea about wrestling – I asked him what his name was. 'Stone Cold Steve Austin,' he replied. Now this name I knew. This name was pasted over cards and sticker books all over our house. This man was your hero. I couldn't speak, I was so excited for you. I wished that you were there to meet him but as you weren't, I did the next best thing. I begged him to call you up and talk to you over the phone and he happily obliged. I put my ear to the phone and listened to your little voice go quiet when he said his name. You couldn't speak and when you did, all you could manage was, 'Alright, Steve? I mean ... Stone? I mean ... Mr Cold?' He spoke to you for a few minutes and when I spoke to Mummy after, she said you were floating on cloud nine and calling all your friends to tell them. I was so happy I'd done this for you, surely I was the coolest big sister in the world now?

I walked over to my friends, proud as punch, and told them what had happened. A few of my boy friends looked over and burst out laughing. They then informed me that it wasn't Steve Austin at all but a good lookalike. He'd conned me. I was heartbroken, not because I looked silly but because of how happy you'd been to speak to your idol. I went home and you were jumping *for joy and, just like the Pradas, I never had the heart to tell you the truth. You lived on that story for the next few years, impressing everyone, and I would simply nod along and smile, feeling like the worst sister ever.*

Now I'm off to meet the Prime Minister and I'm scared. You wouldn't be. You wouldn't even be impressed – he's no Steve Austin, that's for sure. But he is only meeting me because of you – the tables have been turned. You're the little 'celebrity' now and maybe if he had been the real thing, that Steve Austin would be walking around now saying, 'I spoke to that Ben Kinsella once.' How cool is that?

When I walked up Downing Street, my legs were shaking. As I passed through all the security gates, petrified of the uniformed men standing there with guns, I couldn't believe I was actually there.

Our house phone had rung a few days earlier, with 'anonymous' displayed on the caller ID. I answered it and a voice asked to speak to me. I was shocked when, after I identified myself, the voice said, 'Could you hold? I have the Home Secretary for you.' I ran around in a panic. I had no idea who the Home Secretary was. I am ashamed to say I've never followed politics, though I was trying to take more of an interest since my brother had died.

I ran up to my mum in a panic and whispered, 'Who's the Home Secretary?' Her face went blank and she hopped around just like me.

'I'll call Dad,' she said, and went running off. Knowing

she would be no help, I went running back down to Jade, who was on the Internet. 'Quick,' I hissed, 'Google the Home Secretary! Find out who it is!' This Home Secretary was going to be on the line any second now and I really didn't want to sound like I had no clue about politics whatsoever.

My mum then came charging in triumphantly and said, 'I've remembered! It's David Blunkett!' I gave her a grateful thumbs up and, that second, a woman's voice came on the line and began talking. She spoke about Ben and how sorry she was, and said that she was also sorry she wouldn't get to meet me when I met Gordon Brown in the next couple of days but she was extremely busy. She told me she was amazed at the good work I'd done and said what an inspiration I was, and I listened and replied politely, all the while wondering who she was and when David Blunkett would be coming to talk to me.

She then wished me luck with everything and put the phone down and I was left standing there confused. Why hadn't I been able to speak to the main man himself? My mum then sheepishly came in and said that David Blunkett hadn't been the Home Secretary for a while and it was now a lady called Jacqui Smith. I had missed my chance to say what I wanted. I wasn't annoyed, as we all cried with laughter over our mistake. It only highlighted how clueless we were – what chance did we have of taking on the government when we couldn't even name them? I was determined to do my homework; however, I only had a short time in which to do it.

A couple of days later, waiting in a private drawing room for the Prime Minister, I remembered my mum hopping around and got a fit of uncontrollable giggles. I prayed that they would go before he came in.

Gordon Brown had kindly allowed our meeting to be filmed by the BBC for my documentary and I had also asked if I could bring my dad along for support. He was sitting there, with a straight back and looking very stern, and I worried that as soon as he walked in, my dad would give Gordon a piece of his mind. However, he turned to me and whispered, 'Do you think we could nick a teaspoon to take back for Mummy?' and my giggles were back.

I had never met a prime minister. I had never wanted to. I saw them as boring old men who pretended to run the country and promised lots of things that we never got. The last time I'd voted I chose the Monster Raving Loony Party, just for a change. It was hypocritical of me really. How could I criticize politicians and parties when I had no real idea who they were or what they did exactly?

I expected Gordon Brown to be stuffy and insensitive, to just say what he thought we wanted to hear and give us five minutes of his time before moving on to bigger and more important things. I was prepared not to like him, I was determined not to like him – I wanted to make him feel bad for what had happened to us.

When he finally walked in the room, the first thing I noticed was his warmth and his presence. That and the fact that he actually looked more nervous than me. He shook all our hands and smiled, and the first thing he said was how sorry he was for our loss. He looked my dad in the eye when he said this and I knew instantly that he had done the right thing. He wasn't shying away or trying to tiptoe round us, he got right to the reason why we were there.

That meeting was such a blur. I had planned over and over in my head what I was going to say but as soon as I was sat there facing him, my carefully planned speech disappeared. I wasn't star-struck or anything but even I knew how powerful this man was, and what an honour it was that he'd taken time out of his extremely busy schedule to meet me.

I told him all about my visit to New York, stuttering and mixing up my words, and he listened patiently. He did that typical politician thing of keeping quiet and nodding, so that you pour your whole heart out in five minutes, and I was impressed. I had been determined to give him a really hard time but he seemed so normal and sympathetic that I found it difficult. I felt guilty – I'd been blaming the government for the state of our country and had wanted a chance to direct all my anger at them and here it finally was . . . only I found I couldn't do it. It wasn't just this one man's fault and at least he was here, listening to what we had to say, asking us for help.

I think what also made him slightly more sensitive than your average politician was that he had lost a child himself.

Not in the cruel, harsh way we had, but he knew what it was like to lose someone you loved and that really showed in his character.

I thought maybe I was just a soft touch but I knew he was a good guy by the fact my dad seemed to like him. My dad is a tough man to please and I knew that he was so angry with the government for allowing things to get this bad, so I fully expected to have to pull him off Gordon Brown and go home to tell my mum he'd been arrested! But he was simply sitting there and opening up, something he never did, and telling Mr Brown what he thought needed to be done.

There was no rush, nobody stood over us making us feel pressured or interrupted us to say 'two more minutes'. We said what we needed to and put our ideas across, and when we'd finished, Gordon told us what actions he and the government had planned.

He reiterated the fact that the penalties for carrying knives had been doubled to four years and I asked him if this was actually being imposed. He said that although the government passed the laws, it was up to the judicial systems to enforce them, but that they were leaning heavily on them to do so. He spoke about advertising and funding and, although it was good news, I'd heard this all before. I wanted to know what else they were doing, what new things they were going to use to try and solve this problem. I'd heard no ideas as good as the boot camp or other nationwide projects that I wanted so badly.

He must have read my mind as he then started to tell us about a national anti-knife campaign the government was planning to launch. He said that instead of being a government-driven project, something that most people disagreed with and didn't believe in, he wanted it to be people-driven. He planned to create a 'steering group', a team of people made up of celebrities, victims, ordinary people, youth workers and so on, who would each work on all the different sections that would be involved in tackling the problem.

He spoke about getting people from the worlds of football, music and film involved. He wanted a brand and a logo, a tag everybody could easily identify with and get behind, and he wanted it to be as big as the 'Kick Racism Out of Football' campaign. It was very early days yet but the first meeting would be held in the next week, where everybody would get the chance to put forward their ideas and come up with solutions together. Once everybody was clear on what needed to be done, it would be launched nationally and the message would finally be clear: 'No More Knives'.

It sounded impressive. It sounded like what I'd been looking for and what we needed. There was no point in having lots of little groups working on their own, trying to change things individually. Yes, every project helped massively and if even one kid was saved, that was good enough, but there were so many amazing people out there with strong ideas that if they all came together and were given the proper platform and opportunity to show what they could do, it might make an even bigger difference.

Gordon Brown was finally listening to the people and allowing them to be in charge and I really hoped he would stick to his word. I knew they'd tried similar projects before but this would only work if they stopped simply trying to *look* as if they were doing something and actually got on and did it. They needed to involve the real people – the people on the streets, the people that were living this nightmare every day – and only then would they find the right answers.

When the meeting was almost over, he turned to me and asked me if I would like to come on board the project and be one of its ambassadors. He wanted me to work closely with the Prince's Trust and help develop a project that could be taken into all the schools to show kids the devastation carrying a knife could cause.

I was speechless. Not only was I extremely proud, I was also excited as I felt this was something I could really do well. I'd taught children for years and found it so reward-ing and if I could help create a project that would change the way kids felt, I would really feel like I'd achieved something. I had so many good ideas incorporating drama and workshops and rehabilitation, and finally felt like I had a direction to head in. I still wanted to get the boot camp idea off the ground, I still really thought it would make such a difference, but at least this was a start. Maybe if we went into schools and got to the kids early, they wouldn't grow up and need to be put into a boot camp, they wouldn't end up in prison.

I immediately accepted the Prime Minister's invitation and went running home to tell my mum. I knew it would be a lot of hard work but I was determined not to be there simply as a face. I wasn't one of the celebrity ambassadors; I was there as someone who had real experience of this problem and I really wanted to give my input and help make this campaign as good as it could be.

The next week, I found myself sitting around a table with footballers such as John Terry and Ashley Cole, the owners of the music awards MOBO, representatives from the social networking site Bebo and the supermarket chain ASDA. There were also people from victim support groups, clergymen, politicians and celebrities.

I didn't even understand what some of the people there could offer until we got going. The support needed from the footballers and musicians and celebrities was clear – they were going to act as role models to the kids out there, they would shout the message 'No to Knives' from the rooftops and would try to make carrying a weapon uncool. It was common knowledge that kids looked up to celebrities and sportspeople more than anyone who was in authority and we hoped that if their favourite idol was telling them to drop the knife, they might do so.

I was amazed at how much support everybody was giving. ASDA had decided not to sell knives online any more, therefore limiting people's access to weapons, and were also going to spread the message in all their stores across the country. Bebo, the popular networking site that had millions of members, were going to set up anti-knife groups where kids could join up to show their support and could also become ambassadors for this scheme. There was no faster way to spread a message than online and we hoped this would make a massive impact.

The MOBO awards were going to try and incorporate awards for deprived kids who'd tried their hardest to make something of themselves, again showing the people out there that it was the kids who worked hard who would be rewarded and not those who took the easy way out. We believed that if kids saw their peers being recognized publicly for outstanding work and achievements, they too would want to show the world what else they could do besides criminal activities. The Prince's Trust and I were going to reach out to all the schools and provide education and awareness. Radio networks and TV stations pledged their support and promised to keep public awareness going – it really seemed like it could work.

There were lots of debates in that first meeting and many, many ideas were thrown about but the one thing we all agreed on, the thing we believed was most important, was that first we had to talk to the people on the streets, and in particular the kids, because they were the ones who really knew what was going on out there.

After that initial meeting, a conference was set up which

would be attended by kids from different schools and colleges across London. The steering group would then go in and sit round tables with these kids and listen to them, in the hope that they could tell us what we needed to know.

I sat on a table with kids as young as eleven, not understanding what they could possibly know about knife crime – surely they were too young? I was wrong. Whatever I'd learned in the past six months was nothing to what these kids knew. They amazed me. They spoke intelligently and sensibly, better than any politician or motivational speaker I'd ever heard.

Opinions were divided – some didn't think prison and tougher sentences helped at all, some said that having been in prison themselves it had changed them for the better. They all agreed that kids needed more time and effort spent on them, more recreational activities, better support systems in school, basically just more attention. In one hour we came up with so many ideas: 'Big Brother' pilot schemes, where people could volunteer to mentor and spend time with kids who had no one else to turn to; work experience placements – we had the bigwigs from sport, music and film on board, which were the paths most young kids dreamed of following. If they could agree to take kids on and give them a taste of what they could achieve if they worked hard enough, maybe it would be a big enough incentive to carry on.

Strangely, one thing that most of the kids wanted was a decent education. They felt that becoming a lawyer or a doctor was impossible, that going to college or university seemed out of the question so, with good careers seemingly being out of their reach, they thought it was easier to make money the illegal way, regardless of the consequences.

It was a surreal experience, being lectured by young children. Looking around, I saw Ashley Cole and John Terry listening intently, the Prime Minister moving from table to table and every kid speaking animatedly, speaking from the heart. All they needed was an audience. Yes, they were star-struck over their heroes and the first half of the conference was taken up by autograph signing and the demanding of photos as souvenirs, but once we got down to business, they didn't care who they were talking to, as long as they were being heard.

At the end of the conference, Gordon Brown thanked everybody and announced the details of the anti-knife campaign to the press, promising that real changes were to come. Everybody left the room with a sense of achievement, and for the first time since my brother died, I really felt as if I'd got somewhere. The problem was no longer being brushed under the carpet; there was no hiding from it any more. Those that carried weapons would soon realize it would no longer be tolerated and although my family could never get Ben back and would be broken forever, I looked forward to the day when this nightmare epidemic was a distant bad memory.

I'd learned a great deal in the past few months and now

needed to reassess my opinions. In the beginning, I'd been adamant that tougher sentencing was the only way to go. I wanted people punished, I wanted them locked up forever in a cell and left to rot. I listened to people's ideas about rehabilitation but I disagreed and disregarded it as a possible solution. In my opinion, being soft would get us nowhere; we had to lay down the law.

Having met so many different people and experienced so many different projects, I had to admit my mind was slowly being changed.

The first time I began to think that harsh punishment was not the way to go, I felt sick with guilt. I really felt like I was betraying my brother, that I wasn't fighting hard enough for him, that I was excusing what had happened to him. Eventually I came to see that this wasn't true and could finally admit that I could see the sense in both schools of thought. I still stuck to my guns and believed that those who'd committed serious crimes needed to be punished justly. Even if I hadn't had my own biased view of this, if my brother hadn't been murdered, I would still be of the same opinion. It isn't fair to take someone's life and not have your own severely impacted.

However, I now understood that many of these crimes may not have happened had there been more care and attention delivered early on. It was too late to help some people, but many kids out there were on the cusp of turning bad and if they didn't get the help they needed, they would hurt themselves or somebody else. Most people may think that it's not their problem, that they've brought their own kids up as best they could so why should they bother with anybody else's children. But, as I found out, one day it could easily become your problem. A kid that may have been led down a better path may continue on the road of destruction and hurt somebody you love and, like me, you'll wish that you'd tried to do something beforehand.

I'd gone on this journey to find answers but also to define my own moral code. It would have been easy just to be hell-bent on getting revenge and to allow myself to express the rage and anger that was within me, but that wasn't me. It wasn't how I'd been brought up, it wasn't the person I was, and to change that would let 'them' win again.

I now knew exactly where I stood and what I believed in. I would never, ever forgive what had been done to my brother. I would never understand it, I would never excuse it and I wanted fair justice for him. Nobody could take that view away from me and I would not apologize for it. I was angry and I wanted just deserts but I would try my hardest to find a better way for the next generation of kids coming up. I only hoped that the government and everybody else who had played a part in creating this culture would learn from their previous mistakes and make the changes they'd promised me and the rest of the country.

I had done all I could. I'd reached the end of my journey and all I could do now was wait to see if any of it was worth it. I really hoped that I hadn't wasted all those months. I hoped that some good, no matter how small, would come from what I'd tried to do.

I now had to get on with the task of grieving, which, for me, was the hardest job of all. It was time to really face up to what had happened, to take a step back and digest everything and to accept that my little brother was gone and never coming back. We had a few months to go until the trial and I decided to use that time to take a break from campaigning and try to find Brooke again. I wanted to spend time with my family, to make sure that we were as prepared as we could be for what were surely to be some of the hardest weeks of our lives, as we finally learned the truth about what had really happened that night.

Chapter 13

I stand in your room and look around it for the last time. I try to memorize every item, every drawing, every little thing that you have collected in your sixteen years of living. Soon it will all be gone, we will all be gone – to a new house where it doesn't break our hearts every time we walk into a room.

Mummy tells us all to take some things of yours to remember you by – the rest will be boxed up and stored away just like you.

I start in your wardrobe, with all your lovely boy clothes that still smell of you, even five months on. It's hard to narrow it down but, in the end, I choose my two favourite jumpers of yours – one that you wore the last Christmas you were here with us and the one that you were wearing the last time I ever saw you, the last one that I ever hugged you in.

I look around, wondering what I could possibly take that will be a good enough substitute for you. I find some theatre tickets from two years ago, for a show that I took you to see, and I can't

---

believe that you've saved them. I'm happy it was a good enough day for you to keep them as a souvenir and if they're good enough for you, they're good enough for me, so I take them.

Your computer and games will go to your beloved friends. Your pictures and cherished football shirts as well. Everybody who wants a little piece of you will have one, as we know this is what you would have wanted.

I don't know what else to take. I don't want things, I just want you. I don't want a new home, I want this one.

I find your bus pass with a photo of you smiling widely and I keep that also. I love seeing you smile and I collect every picture that has you doing so, storing them away as a cure for when I break down crying.

I see your superhero underpants on your rocking chair, lying there where you left them all those months ago. Nobody has had the heart to move them. I hold them up and can't believe how small they are, can't believe you were really that skinny. You never stood a chance.

Finally, as I go to leave, I look up on your toiletry shelf. I debate whether to take some aftershave to remind me of your smell, but there's hardly any left – every bottle is nearly empty, which isn't surprising with the amount you splashed on every day, always trying to impress the ladies.

At the back, I spy your toothbrush and gently take it down, amazed that I nearly walked away without this treasure. I know you will be cracking up, looking down and wondering why on earth I would want your manky old toothbrush, but I am one step ahead of you, little brother, for if they are ever able to clone *humans properly in my lifetime, I'll have something that may be able to bring you back to us.*

I put it carefully in a carrier bag and add it to the rest of my 'Ben Box'. This is a place that I will go to when the pain of missing you becomes too much, when I start to doubt if you were ever really here. I will have your jumpers to keep me warm and comfort me, your smiling face and our memories to cheer me up and, best of all, a manky old toothbrush to make a wish on. It's not a good enough substitute but it's better than nothing.

After six months, the pain of living in a house without Ben became too much to bear. My parent's bedroom was opposite Ben's and every morning they had to wake up and look into their son's empty room, a haunting reminder to them that he would never be coming home again.

My mum finally decided she couldn't take it any more and begged the council to move us. She didn't want to go far as Georgia was still in school and it was unfair to uproot her after everything that had happened. In the early days, we even spoke about moving to another country but decided we wanted to stay close to where Ben was buried and where the streets were still full of memories of him. My mum didn't want to move but said that she needed to get out of that house if she was ever to be able to attempt to get over what had happened.

If I was honest, I didn't want to move either. Even though I was meant to be moving out the day Ben had died, I wasn't ready and things were different now. We'd already lost Ben, I didn't want to lose the rest of my family and our memories too. It was hard walking around the house and seeing him everywhere but it was better than the alternative. I didn't want to move to a new house that Ben had never lived in, that he'd never even seen. It felt so wrong to be leaving him behind. I worried that if we moved and he came looking for us, he wouldn't be able to find us. Silly, I know, but I couldn't bear the thought of him coming to visit only to find an empty house and all his family gone.

I wanted to stay in the house that we'd all grown up in together and that had held such happy memories for us all up until recently. It didn't seem fair that after everything we had gone through, we had to leave our lovely home as well.

However, it was ultimately my parents' decision and I soon came to realize they'd made the right one. I'd been selfish in wanting to keep everything the same. If moving house was what it took to make them feel even a tiny bit better, then I would happily do so. As long as we were all still together, that was all that mattered.

However, the house that was eventually found for us only had two bedrooms and a tiny box room, meaning that Jade and I would have to find places of our own. I already had my own place that was currently lying empty, but that wasn't the point. This was the last straw for me. In the space of six months we'd gone from a loving family of six to being separated and scattered around and I found it so unfair. We may have been able to escape from the pain of Ben's empty room but it came at a heavy cost, as now there would be two more empty rooms. People said that it didn't matter because Jade and I would have moved out on our own eventually, but it did matter. It wasn't the same when you didn't have a choice, when you were forced into it. I couldn't act like a spoiled brat, though, because it meant so much to my parents, so I kept quiet and resigned myself to the fact that I'd be living on my own.

I couldn't believe how much our lives had changed in just a few short months. It was like everything was topsy-turvy and I didn't know if I was coming or going, or if anything would ever feel safe and stable again.

The day finally came when we had to pack up and leave. My mum had done most of the work – I simply couldn't face it and cried every time I tried to box up my stuff. None of us had the energy to do much and in the end we simply left most of our belongings there, preferring to start again. If we were going to try and start afresh, we might as well do it properly.

The worst thing was leaving all the drawings and paintings that Ben had done on his bedroom walls. There was a life-size caricature that he'd done of himself and we all loved it but couldn't think of a way to bring it with us. In the end we took a photo of it and resigned ourselves that that was the closest we would get to keeping it. A couple of weeks after moving into the new house, a family friend knocked on the door with a present for us. It was bigger than all of us and extremely heavy and we couldn't think for a moment what it could be. My mum tore the wrapping paper off and stared at it in disbelief. Standing there was an exact copy of Ben's caricature. 'It looks just like the real thing!' she said in amazement.

'It is the real thing!' laughed our friend.

He'd gone back to the old house, sneaked in and cut a hole in the wall to remove Ben's painting. He'd then had it beautifully framed. We all cried tears of happiness and thanked him but all my mum could worry about was the hole in the wall and whether we would get in trouble for vandalizing.

Again, we couldn't have done anything without our friends and they all rallied round to help until finally the door was locked and there was no going back. My family moved into a house just around the corner from our old one and I moved into my flat ten minutes away.

The first few weeks on my own were tough. I went back to my mum's nearly every day and although they were more than happy to have me there, I knew that I'd have to be on my own sooner or later.

For me, the scariest thing in the world was being on my own. I'd always been a baby anyway, but now I was a complete wreck. My boyfriend Ray had moved in with me to keep an eye on me but if he went out for the night or needed to stay at his own place, I couldn't handle it. Before, I'd been scared of ghosts and monsters – even at the age of twenty-five I was too scared to get out of bed in the middle of the night to get a drink – but now the only thing I was scared of was myself.

When I was on my own, dark and horrible thoughts would creep into my brain. With nothing and no one to distract me, I would hear my brother crying and screaming, I would try to re-enact his last moments, I would torment myself over and over again until it got to the point where I just wanted to make it all stop.

However, I never let it get to the point of doing something stupid – I'd made that decision a while back and was determined to stick to it, but it went far enough that it constantly seemed as if I was about to have a breakdown. For the first few months, I couldn't even have sharp knives or painkillers in my flat because I was just too scared that in the depths of my nightmares I would try to use them.

It was my mum, as always, who helped me. I was simply looking at my flat as a temporary stop-off, a place I was just staying in until I went back to my real home with my family. I took no pride in it and didn't even try to make it homely. I was too busy concentrating on my old life and memories to bother to make new ones.

Mum convinced me that making the flat my own would make everything much better. She said that I could come home and live with them if I really wanted to but that if I was ever going to try and make it on my own, now was the best time, as if I could get through this, I could get through anything. She and my dad spent weeks decorating my flat on a budget – painting and building until eventually it turned from a shell that was cold and empty to a home that was colourful and cosy.

They did all this while decorating their own new house and getting everyone settled in as best they could. Although they were constantly running around and busy, the good thing was that it distracted them and gave them something else to think about for a little while.

When I tried to tell them to take a break and that they didn't have to get everything finished at once I was ignored. I think this was partly because, just like me and my work, they were scared to stop. They'd realized that keeping busy helped a great deal and would rather be exhausted than sitting around with too much time to think. The most important thing they needed to get everything ready for though was the next 'first' occasion, and the hardest one we would ever have to face – our first Christmas without Ben.

Everything up until then had been a struggle. His funeral, his birthday, our birthdays – things that used to be joyous occasions for us were now some of the most depressing days of our lives. Nothing, however, can explain just how hard it was to get through our first Christmas with one of us missing.

Christmas in our house had always been a typical family affair. Jade and I would go out Christmas Eve with friends and dread it when at seven o'clock the next morning Ben and Georgia would come running in to wake us up. Ben still jumped up early with excitement even when he got older and I suspect that had he lived a long life, he would have continued to do this every year, no matter how old he was.

Ben adored presents. He wasn't selfish or greedy or spoiled – he just absolutely loved opening presents, that or being given money to spend, and I loved buying presents for him as he was always so thankful and happy. He also always gave something back and the month before he died, he'd spent his whole week's wages on a birthday present for my sister, leaving himself with nothing but not caring.

We all had our own 'present' spot in the living room, it had been that way for as long as I could remember, and every Christmas Eve, my mum would sort everybody's presents into piles where they would be waiting for us the next morning. After lots of 'oohs' and 'aahs' and 'thank-yous', we'd all clean up and change into our new pyjamas, which was another tradition. Then us kids would laze about and watch films while Dad went to the pub for a pint and Mum cooked dinner, often with Ben as her assistant chef. Not only did my mum decide to give the long eyelash genes to the only boy, she also gave him all the cooking skills too. At sixteen, he was truly a genius. He would watch cooking programmes all day long and memorize the recipes, then recreate them with his own twist. He put me and Jade to shame – the best I could do was boil pasta – and when I moaned that I was starving and there was nothing to eat, he'd rummage around in the fridge and produce a meal fit for a king out of thin air. Granted, he absolutely destroyed the kitchen while he did so, but the end result was always so nice that it was worth the cleaning up. Despite his skill, he never wanted to pursue a career as a chef, the reason being that he hated red meat and fish and therefore wouldn't be able to taste most of the dishes he created.

He even managed to make Brussels sprouts nice and on Christmas Day would take over from my mum, rolling them around in bacon and honey until they were actually things of beauty.

We'd all sit down together, pulling crackers, making jokes and arguing about who would do the washing up. This was always settled with family games after dinner, though even if the kids won, we'd still be forced to clean up – it was, after all, the least we could do.

Our Christmases were nothing special, no different from any other families' and hardly worth writing about. Although it was my favourite day of the year, I almost took it for granted and last year moaned that we should do something different, go abroad or something, just have a change.

I never wanted this kind of change though. If I'd known that Christmas the year before would be Ben's last one, I'd have cherished every moment. I'd have bought him everything he'd ever wanted, would have fattened him up and given him triple helpings, let him choose what we watched, what we played . . . I would have made sure that it was his best Christmas ever. We weren't lucky enough to be forewarned, though, and I'd asked for change and got it.

This Christmas, not only were we missing someone, we were in a completely new house and it was so sad and strange. We'd only been there a month and my mum had done amazing things but it still didn't really feel like home. We had discussed going abroad to get away from everything but, as it was all Ben had ever wanted us to do at Christmas, it didn't feel fair to do it without him, especially as he had only been gone a few months.

We then discussed completely ignoring it altogether, closing the curtains and shutting the door and locking the cheer and the Christmas spirit out. The build-up over the past few weeks had been awful and although it was nobody else's fault or problem, I couldn't stand seeing people happy and smiling, seeing other families having fun just like we used to. When friends of mine discussed what presents they'd buy for their little brothers or sisters, I wanted to scream at them just to shut up, but of course that was selfish and unfair.

It was also unfair on Georgia to completely ignore Christmas – not that she particularly wanted to celebrate it, but we couldn't all just give up and hide away. We knew Ben would want us to do what we did every year and celebrate it for him and so we tried our hardest. We all put on brave faces and prepared to get through the day, though it was extremely hard. Instead of jumping up at seven as usual, we all lay in bed crying quietly before coming down to breakfast. There was no rush to open our presents, no excitement, and the tiny little piles were nothing compared to what we usually gave each other. We couldn't face opening them until the afternoon and although nobody even wanted anything, we still all got little tokens of love. I bought everyone beautiful canvases and framed pictures of Ben, which set them all off and made me feel bad.

My mum cooked her usual amazing dinner and although we didn't have any special Brussels sprouts, it was better than anyone expected. We said a toast to Ben at the table and prayed that God would let him come and visit and be with us, just for that day.

Then we did something that in all our Christmases we had never done before – we went our separate ways. Georgia and Jade went out with friends, my dad went to the pub and I went out for a drink. The simple truth was that we couldn't put on those brave faces any longer. Being around each other and seeing how heartbroken we were hurt us all too much. It was easier to go out, to be around other 'normal' people, to not have to be strong any more.

I briefly wondered what Christmas was like for those who had killed my brother. Did they get Christmas dinner in prison? Were they allowed to open presents from their families, allowed to see and hug and kiss their families?

Did they stop for one second on that day that was made just for families and think about what they'd done to mine?

And what about Ben? I wondered how his Christmas was going – whether he was up there having the time of his life or looking down on us sadly, wishing he could join in. Wishing that none of this had happened so he could be with us playing games and laughing like normal.

There'd been many dark days in the past few months but that one was the worst. I watched my mum hold it together all day and then, once everybody had gone out and it was safe to do so, lose the plot completely. For two hours solid she sobbed her heart out and I was so scared, I didn't know whether to call a doctor or a priest. I couldn't even make out the words she was saying but could see the complete grief and anger in her eyes and could do nothing to help. She'd been so strong but even the strongest person in the world would have a hard time coping when they had to visit their son's grave on Christmas Day.

We'd all gone to see him after breakfast, noticing other people had taken time out of their special day to visit him and keep him company. Unlike his birthday, we didn't bring him any cards or buy him any presents, we simply sat there on the cold and icy ground and cried and cried before going home to eat a wonderful dinner none of us could taste. How my mum had managed to make it through the day I will never know. She finally calmed down, not because she wanted to but because she had to. She was a mum and mums always pull themselves together.

We were nearly at the end of our 'firsts'. There was only New Year and Mother's and Father's Day left to get through and although I knew that all of the 'special' days would be hard to get through over the coming years, I truly dreaded Christmas coming back round as I knew that it would never, ever, get any easier.

Part of me didn't want it to, either. I didn't want to get to the point where it stopped hurting, where I could smile fondly at memories and be glad that at least I'd had him at all. I didn't want in years to come to say, 'I remember when I had a brother, twenty, thirty years ago . . .' Time was flying by quickly, half a year had already gone and, before we knew it, he'd have been gone for longer than he'd ever been here. I dreaded that day.

New Year's Eve came and went with more tears and more heartache. 2009 was a year that Ben had never been a part of, would never know anything about – he was already history. The stroke of midnight on New Year's Eve is symbolic. It represents a change, a new start, better times ahead. I had looked forward to every New Year and used to pray that this one would be my time, that it was when all my wishes would come true.

Now, all I wanted was to go back. I didn't want any more changes, I didn't have any wishes to be fulfilled, I simply wanted to stop time and be frozen in a year that my brother had been alive in.

Why Ben?

Now that I had nothing to keep me busy and nothing to do, the grief and the depression was starting to kick in and everything I had held at a distance so far came rushing forward. Even though it was over half a year on, it felt as if I was back at square one. The pain was so great, it was as if Ben had only just died, and for the next couple of months, I turned into an angry, uncontrollable monster. On the surface I seemed strong and together but, behind closed doors, I really felt as if I was sinking into a dark hole that I would never come out of.

Chapter 14

I am angry all the time. I am angry at everyone – at them, at myself, sometimes even at you. When I'm at my lowest and have no one left to blame, I cry and turn to you. Why did you go out that night? Why didn't you stay in, in the warm where it was safe, why did you run, why did you cross the road, why you? Then I hate myself and want to punish myself and I cry even more.

Of course I'm not angry at you, it wasn't your fault, you did nothing wrong apart from be in the wrong place at the wrong time and I hope you know this. I hope that you're not up there blaming yourself, worrying that you've caused us all to hurt so much, worrying that it was all your fault. I can't bear to think of you being upset or angry, you've been through enough and there was nothing you could have done – there's nothing any of us could have done.

I can't get your last moments out of my head. I'm tired of making them up. I just want to know the truth, I want to know what you were feeling, what you were thinking.

———

Did you lie in the ambulance scared and hurting or did you fall into a restful sleep, not really knowing what had happened? Did you worry that when you got home you were going to be in trouble and would probably get grounded for causing all this bother? Did you know it was really bad, that there was a chance you might not make it, did you feel it when you were about to die? They say that bright light surrounds you, that people come to get you and look after you, that God speaks to you – did this happen, were you ready, or did you cry when you knew you had to go?

Did you know that we were downstairs praying? That we were there, that you weren't on your own at the end. Did it hurt when it finally happened or were you relieved to be rid of the pain?

Do you know that every one of us would swap places with you if we could and that there isn't one second of every day when I don't wish that it had been me instead?

Do you know how empty our lives are without you or do you look down and catch us on the rare occasions we're smiling or laughing and think that we're doing OK, that we're getting over it and forgetting about you?

We will never forget you, Ben. You may have been here only a short while, but you filled our lives with so much love and happiness that you will be imprinted on our hearts forever, no matter how many years go by. I hope you know that. I really do.

The months leading up to the trial were a hard time for me. Although I'd decided to take some time out and try to

_____

deal with things, I couldn't take the pain and immediately wanted to go back to work on the campaign, to do anything to take my mind off what had happened. This wasn't an option, though, as I'd been placed under a strict media and campaigning ban. With the trial coming up, the police thought it was unwise to keep highlighting Ben and putting him in the spotlight, as they believed this could jeopardize his trial. If the public kept hearing about Ben they would probably all be sympathetic to his case and therefore, when it came to picking members of a jury or giving the accused a fair trial, it would be tough. Although I understood this logic, to me it seemed as if, again, those that were accused had all the rights. Everything was being done to protect them, to give them a fair trial, while my family were hiding away, petrified to talk to anybody in case we said the wrong thing. Sometimes it seemed as if we were the ones who'd done something bad. Although the police tried to keep us updated as much as possible, there were some things they couldn't tell us before the trial in case it got out, so we always felt as if we were in the dark and everybody else knew something that we didn't. We knew that my brother would have witnesses standing up for him but we weren't allowed to know who they were. This was hard as we lived in such a small community, where everybody knew each other, that it was hard not to hear things or stop ourselves asking questions.

I began to get very down and depressed and it didn't help that I had nothing to do all day. I started going back to auditions but didn't seem to be having any luck and I couldn't blame the directors for not giving me the parts – I'd let myself go, I didn't care about my appearance or my health and also, I didn't really want to get a job as I wanted to be at the trial every day so didn't see the point of auditioning. This attitude obviously showed and stopped me from getting work, which made me even more upset.

It was like a vicious cycle – I had nothing to get up for and so I simply lay around the house, one minute crying and the next flying into angry rages.

Ray tried to help me but – obviously, with him being the closest to me – I took everything out on him and he found it hard to deal with. Ray and my friends had been brilliant at keeping me occupied and cheering me up but they had their own lives to live and couldn't keep taking days off work or going out every night to keep me company. As unfair as I knew it was, I began to resent everyone around me. I hated them for having lives and dreams and ambitions. I hated them for having complete families and for moaning about silly arguments with siblings or parents or crying over rows with partners. I tried to listen and be the good friend I used to be but inside I was screaming at how pointless and petty it all was and I wanted to tell them what real hurt and pain felt like.

I became selfish and angry and although I wanted to stop, to go back to being the old Brooke, I didn't know how. I watched my mum and dad argue with each other and begin to fall apart, I watched my sisters slowly become more and more withdrawn and suddenly it was all too much. I couldn't take any more.

I don't really remember what happened – Ray filled in the gaps for me after – but on the day that I finally snapped, we were having an argument that I had started, as always. I was angry, I was hurting and I remember sobbing and not being able to stop, even to breathe. I remember kicking my wardrobe and various bits of furniture and being unable to speak or get out the words I desperately needed to say. I just wanted to make it all stop. Apparently, I then went into the kitchen and picked up a knife and tried to lock myself in the bathroom with it. I'm not sure what I was going to do as I can't remember doing this, but luckily Ray was able to take it off me and calm me down. When he told me later what I'd done, I knew something had to change. I couldn't keep hurting the people around me, or myself, any more. I couldn't keep blaming and resenting others or pushing them away because I would need all the help I could get in the coming weeks. My brother wouldn't want to see me like this so I had to fix myself up.

My decision to snap out of it and get stronger couldn't have come at a better time as, a few weeks before the trial, the police asked us if we would like to see the CCTV footage they had of the night Ben had died and the autopsy reports describing his wounds. Obviously this evidence was sacred but it would all be brought up at the trial and they wanted to prepare us first, so that we wouldn't have to see or hear it for the first time in front of dozens of people. It was our decision but there was only ever one answer. No matter how hard it would be viewing the CCTV footage, nothing could be worse than the terrifying images I conjured up in my own mind and I wanted to know the truth. I knew that he had received eleven wounds but, even months on, we only knew where a few of them were and all I could think was, where were the rest? What if they'd got him in his little misters? I couldn't bear not knowing.

We drove to the police headquarters and, after meeting the head detective, who gave us a brief update, we were shown around and introduced to the team working on Ben's case. We were then taken down to the viewing room and, as we sat there holding hands, the tape began to play.

Unfortunately, there wasn't much on there. I'd spent weeks preparing myself for this, believing that I would finally see for myself just what had happened but this wasn't the case.

At the beginning of the tape, we could see my brother and the group of boys he was with walking up the road towards the camera. We then saw them begin to run, obviously realizing they were being chased. I saw Ben's skinny arms and legs pumping away and willed him to run faster, begged him to make it away safely, even though I knew there could only be one outcome. We saw my brother stop and cross over to the other side of the road and this is where his luck ran out. Not only did crossing over the road enable him to get caught and killed, but the camera was a panning one and in the short matter of time it took for them to do what they did, the camera had turned around and was filming the other side of the road. By the time it panned back, it was all over and the only thing it caught was my brother standing up and walking out from behind a van, covered in blood and looking down at himself as if he was unable to believe what had happened. We saw him look to his left, presumably in the direction that his attackers had run off in and shake his head, as if he was so disappointed. He then slowly began to walk away. He didn't run, he didn't collapse or crawl, he simply walked away and if it wasn't for the dark stains on his shirt, you could almost believe he was OK. He then walked out of shot and that was the last we saw of him.

Although we didn't see the actual stabbing, for me it was worse. I will never forget my brother shaking his little head and sadly walking away and I couldn't help but break down crying – in front of the police, in front of my family – I didn't care. That awful image played over and over in my head and will probably do so for the rest of my life.

We were then asked if we still wanted to see the autopsy report and, although I was already distraught, I felt I had to see it. It was better to get everything over and done with at once and I needed to put my mind at rest.

As expected, the report was a lot of medical words and terms that we could barely understand but what was simple for anybody to see was the extent of my brother's injuries. As we already knew, he had been stabbed in his lungs, in his chest and in his stomach, with the fatal blow being that to his heart. The rest of his wounds were given to his arms and his hands, and by the way they were made the police described them as 'self-defence' wounds, meaning he had been struggling to get away.

This was the final blow and dashed any hopes I had of my brother being unconscious when this had happened to him. I was praying that he'd been dazed or stunned and so wouldn't have realized what was going on, but I now knew that he did and that he had tried to push them off, tried to get away, tried to stay alive. If my heart was broken before it was nothing to how I felt now. The only thing I was thankful for was that they hadn't got him in his privates, for I couldn't bear to think of him going through that pain and humiliation also.

Although we left that day knowing a little bit more, we didn't know much and would have to wait until the trial started in a few weeks' time to learn anything else.

The only job we had left to do was to write a family impact statement that would be read out to the court before the sentencing, if they were found guilty. This statement would explain the suffering and pain that had been caused to us and just what life without Ben was like. It was a fairly new thing in the judicial system and its aim was to give the victims and their families some rights, but the sad thing was that the people who were convicted, the people who most needed to hear those heartfelt words, often didn't bother to turn up and listen to it, and that was their right. In the recent Robert Knox case, his family had written a wonderful statement only to find out that the boy who'd been found guilty wasn't even going to be in court to hear it. It seemed so unfair. Even though a statement wasn't going to alter anything, wouldn't change their minds or their actions, it could at least give them an insight into what they had really done.

My mum wrote the statement, as although we could all have written beautiful words about Ben that went on forever, only a mum could really explain the devastation of losing a child. It felt like so much pressure, it felt like we had one chance to tell the world just what they'd done to us, and we wanted to get it right. When we were as happy as we could be with it, we handed it into the police and all we could do then was sit back and wait for everything to start, for the final part of the ordeal to begin.

It was like waiting in limbo. Mother's Day came and went, producing more tears as we all watched my mum trying to struggle through. We all went for dinner and tried to make her day special but it wasn't the same, and although she tried her best for her daughters as always, you could see that all she really wanted was a hug and a kiss from her son.

The one shining bit of light in those dark weeks was when Ben and my family received an award for being a 'Children's Champion'. There had been various ceremonies that had offered an award to myself or to my family over the past few months, and they were often nominated and voted for by the public. Although it was such an honour and we were very grateful to be thought of, we were reluctant to accept any awards because we didn't feel we were any different from any other family that had lost a child to knife crime. I may have been doing some campaigning work but there were many others who were doing a lot more and had been for a lot longer, so I didn't think it was fair to be singled out.

However, the *News of the World*'s Children's Champion award was different. For one thing, it wasn't just my family receiving the award but three – ourselves, the Mizens and the Taylors – and secondly, it wasn't just for the families but also for the children we had lost, the ones who had really made the impact. I could turn down an award for myself but there was no way I could turn away one for Ben.

On the day of the awards, I went back to Downing Street to meet many other nominees and winners, all with amazing stories and who'd all done some truly remarkable things. That evening, I accepted the award on behalf of my family from His Royal Highness Prince Andrew and Richard Taylor gave a marvellous speech on behalf of us and all the other families who had lost someone. I took my two sisters with me and for once they smiled and enjoyed themselves, clapping along to the music and accepting people's apologies and praise. It was an amazing evening and although I still didn't feel I deserved the award and praise, I was so happy that Ben was being recognized as I really felt that he had earned it.

The award took pride of place in our living room and we cherish it – it's a symbol of the support and love that has been given to us by everybody out there.

Although I couldn't wait for the trial to start, a small part of me didn't want it to come around as I felt that once it was completed, everything would be over. There would be nothing left to look forward to, nothing left to fight for. Ben's case would be done and dusted, the file closed, the story finished. He would no longer be in the news, people would begin to forget about him and soon he would be a distant memory. Of course, it shouldn't have mattered if other people forgot him, for all that mattered was that his family and loved ones didn't, but to me it did. I wanted *everyone* to remember him, I wanted his name and his memory to keep on living and I was scared that once the trial was over, so too would be the memory of Ben. It had already been delayed by a week and a selfish part of me hoped that it would be delayed forever, just so it would never be the end. I was also worried about the effects of the trial on us all – having to attend court every day, having to face the press, face the families of those who were accused, was going to be hard and I wished we didn't have to go through it. However, without a trial we would never have the truth and Ben would never get his justice.

Why Ben?

By the time the trial finished he would have been gone almost a year. I couldn't believe how quickly the time had gone, for it often felt like I'd kissed him goodbye only yesterday. By now, he would be almost eighteen, he would have grown even taller and broader and would have become a proper man with dreams and hopes and ambitions.

I didn't know what the coming weeks would bring. If we didn't get the verdict we wanted, I was scared what it would do to us all, but especially to my parents. Although obviously I didn't want anybody to walk free and needed to see someone punished for what had happened to Ben, I also understood that a guilty verdict wasn't going to change anything and wasn't going to bring him back, but it seemed as if we were all waiting for a magic cure, that once we heard the truth and someone was found guilty, we would all feel much better.

I knew this wasn't going to happen though. I also knew that there was a good chance we wouldn't find out anything, that it was possible nobody would be found guilty of Ben's murder and that our worlds could soon fall apart all over again. I was worried that the strength my family had shown so far would crumble and that the last bit of hope and belief we had left would be destroyed.

Chapter 15

I found some home videos of you today. You are a baby, four years old, and skating on the ice rink with Daddy while we all laugh at how wobbly you both are, and you smile that beautiful smile back and wave to the camera.

You're five or six and it looks like it's your birthday party and again you're trying to make everybody laugh – pulling funny faces, pretending you're a monkey and dancing around. Your voice is high and squeaky and your face is round and chubby but it's still you. Those qualities you had later on were present even then and it's strange that we have to go backwards to find them, for we can never go forwards now.

You're seven and playing football, taking it very seriously, shaking hands with everyone afterwards and saying, 'Good game, good game' like a little old man. You're covered in dirt and bruises but smiling proudly because at least you got to kick the ball.

We jump to when you're fourteen or fifteen and painting the

Why Ben?

kids' club at our family's holiday home with your friend, both of you doing it out of the goodness of your hearts, though you've covered yourselves in paint and make up a stupid dance that ends with you both pulling your pants down and doing a moonie to the camera. You're so proud of your choreography that you post this one on the Internet for all to see.

It's shortly before you die and you're outside on a hot summer's day with your friends. Your hair is ruffling in the breeze, those freckles are clear on your face and you're smiling as always. You perform your favourite party trick – stuffing a whole slice of pizza into your mouth at once – and everyone is disgusted but in hysterics when you finally manage it. Only then you can't get it back out and you collapse into giggles and it's the best sound I've heard in a long time. I had forgotten how beautiful your laugh is, how happy it makes people feel. The film stops just as you go to speak, so I can't quite hear how your voice sounded then and, although I can remember sometimes, it's fuzzy and distorted and this upsets me. There's no record of your voice. These are the only videos we have of you – five videos in sixteen years – and I don't understand why we didn't document every single thing you ever did, every achievement you ever made, every second you made us laugh or made us proud.

Maybe because there were too many. Obviously because we didn't know what would happen, but it's too late now and these will have to do. I play them over and over again and each time I hope that they will last just a little bit longer, hope that something will change – like when you used to look in the fridge and you knew there was nothing you liked in there but you'd try *every ten minutes just in case. I'm hoping that the tapes will carry on, that there will be new footage that I've never seen, that I'll discover more to my brother than I already know. But it's just not possible and I stop watching because I worry that the tapes might eventually wear out and that simply can't happen. They have to last us forever.*

The trial for my brother's murder started at the Old Bailey on 27 April 2009. It had been a long time coming and the amount of time and effort that had been put into it was amazing – I could only pray that it was all worth it. We were told by the police that Ben's trial alone would cost almost four million pounds – multiply that amount by the twenty-seven teenagers who were knifed to death just in London that same year and you begin to see the enormity of what this problem is doing to our country.

My family had previously been shown around the Old Bailey in order to prepare us for the coming weeks. We had also met the team of lawyers who were going to be representing us, representing Ben. However, no amount of preparation could have enabled us to be ready for that first day. While we tried to battle the storm of media that surrounded the doors to the court, I realized that this trial was going to be huge and that so, so much would rest on the eventual outcome.

It's astonishing just how many procedures and technicalities there are in cases such as these. This seems like a naive thing to say when you're talking about the law, but when you're dealing with the murder of someone close to you, when you've spent the past year breaking your heart and living in a state of heightened emotion, it seems strange that all those feelings and emotions have to be put aside. They have no place in the courtroom; there is no time for the thoughts of the devastated family, or even to learn about the victim – all anybody is interested in is getting their own stories and points across by any means possible. It's like a game or sport, a competition of who can deliver the best shot, only the outcome is my family's sanity.

The first day was taken up with formalities: introducing the judge, Brian Barker – the Common Serjeant of London – who was the second-highest judge at that time in the Central Criminal Court; producing the defendants, Braithwaite, Alleyne and Kika, officially indicting them and introducing their teams of lawyers, all of whom I hated on sight. I knew they were only doing their jobs, and that this is what they are paid handsomely to do, but I couldn't understand how they could represent cold-blooded murderers and be able to sleep soundly at night. I found out, throughout the course of the trial, that many of them had children of their own and this shocked me. When the whole country was talking about how horrific Ben's murder was, when everybody was disgusted at the epidemic of knife crime and were crying out for the people who used knives to be locked away, how could they possibly tell their families that they were fighting to keep them on the streets? And what did their families think? Were they proud? If they got a not-guilty verdict for the men accused of my brother's murder would they get a pat on the back and a celebratory hug? It didn't make sense to me. If, God forbid, something like this ever happened to one of their own, would they then be so quick to defend the accused?

The most important task on that first day was selecting the jury, which was both fascinating and petrifying to watch. The people chosen would play the biggest part in this whole charade. My brother's justice would lie in the hands of twelve completely random strangers and, looking at them lined up waiting to be called, I couldn't help but judge them. Did that one have children herself? Would he be more sympathetic to the defendants because he was young and black? Would any of them have seen the media coverage and have formed their own opinions already? All possibly unfounded worries, because the jury is ordered to be impartial and to judge the case fairly, but I couldn't help wonder. It's impossible to erase somebody's morals and experiences and it's also very hard not to let these morals and experiences affect your decisions, so I was scared. I hoped that our jury would be sensible and unbiased – even though it could go the other way and be biased in our favour. Yet, strangely, I didn't want that either. Whatever the verdict, I wanted it done properly. There could be no room for mistakes.

After many of the potential jurors had been called up

and had made excuses as to why they couldn't attend the trial – most of them said they couldn't take that much time off work, although I was sure a number of them just didn't want the responsibility that came with this case – we finally had our twelve jurors. At first I was worried because there were many more men than women, but again I was prejudging and I soon realized that there seemed to be a wide range of backgrounds, ages and ethnic groups, which could only be a good thing. Finally, the jury was sworn in, the defendants were put in the dock, and the trial began.

The trial produced vast amounts of information, and each day I came out with my head pounding and my thoughts swimming. What I do remember clearly was that the second I heard the opening speech of our lawyer, Mr Hilliard QC, I knew those three men were guilty of my brother's murder. I had been sure of it all along, but had wanted it confirmed, had wanted it recognized in the eyes of the law, had wanted to see the proof and hear the evidence myself. In all honesty, that first speech was enough for me.

Listening to all the evidence the police had gathered against them – the eyewitnesses, the CCTV footage, and the forensics – it seemed like the case was open and shut then and there. However, the icing on the cake was a series of covert recordings the police had obtained from the defendants in an operation that was a stroke of genius.

In the early days of the accused being arrested, the police already had some evidence against them but needed more. They took a great risk and decided to transport all three defendants to and from the various courts and ID parades together in the same van. While they were driving, they secretly recorded everything the defendants were saying – even pretending the van had broken down and stopping numerous times to ensure they got enough material. The men didn't disappoint: the things that came out of their mouths were vile but invaluable.

The police had mentioned these recordings to us before and we hadn't really understood the enormity of them, but when in the first few days the defendants' legal teams began arguing and tried to stop them being submitted, we knew they must be important. Thankfully, the judge allowed almost all of the dialogue to be admitted as evidence and when the hours of tapes were read out in court, everybody, from my family to the members of the press, was disgusted.

Not only did they speak about how they had committed the murder, they discussed getting rid of knives, made up alibis for each other, planned to 'sort out' any potential witnesses and even laughed and joked around as if it all meant nothing to them, as if what they had done was one big joke. It was sickening to hear them describe how they had killed my brother, saying it was a 'quick ting, go down the road, boom boom, ghost, back up'. 'Ghost', as we found out, meant 'gone' or 'dead', so they knew instantly what they had done that night. They'd intended to kill someone all along.

They planned their alibis together, albeit very sneakily, as if they were aware somebody could be listening in. They were better actors than me. At times they seemed wary of any officers that popped into the van and even questioned whether they were being recorded, but they weren't intelligent enough to keep their mouths shut; they couldn't help bragging about what they'd done. Whatever their reasons for mouthing off, it was priceless for our case.

Two of the defendants, Kika and Alleyne, spoke about how they'd tried to escape from the police the night they were arrested, laughing about jumping from roofs and hiding in bushes, as if it was all a big game. In fact, Kika couldn't stop laughing and joking – while he was in the van he acted like a clown, rapped and sang, even broke wind and checked out girls through the window – all while discussing my brother as if he were nothing but a minor irritation.

While Alleyne and Kika spoke about what happened freely, Jade Braithwaite seemed the most paranoid of the three. Instantly he began questioning the other two over how they had been caught, what evidence they knew of and what stories or lies they planned to tell. At one point he asked that if things got sticky and 'depending on the evi', would they lie for him and pretend he'd been nowhere near them that night? He spoke about two other friends whom he planned to be backed up by and promised that if they lied for him, or if something happened to them and they got 'a couple of years' bird', his aunt and his mum would pay them 'big Gs' – thousands of pounds. Later he tried to say that he had just been boasting and had made this up, and that his family had never intended to pay a witness or hand over any money.

It showed their mentality and how aware they were of the seriousness of their crime, yet it also showed what they thought of the judicial system. Braithwaite knew they were all looking at a jail term – not something you think about if you are actually innocent – but he seriously believed the courts would only lock him and his accomplices away for a 'couple of years'. However untrue this was, if the people committing these crimes believe this is the punishment they will receive, it's no wonder people are being brutally murdered every day.

After listening to those tapes, I believed they should have been convicted on the spot. It seemed farcical to waste everybody's time and the taxpayer's money when it was so clear they were guilty – but of course they had to be given a fair trial.

We then moved on to the many witnesses there had been that night, not of the actual murder unfortunately, but of the events leading up to it – those who had been in Shillibeers bar and had witnessed Braithwaite getting involved in a fight and becoming aggressive; those who had been walking along the street in which my brother was murdered and had seen the three defendants chasing a group of boys, which included Ben; those who had seen them reach my brother, kick him to the ground then disappear from view as they crouched down to attack him. It went on and on. People saw the defendants run away from the scene and meet up to confer about what they had done. Alleyne and Kika were seen running into Alleyne's house while Braithwaite was seen running off down the road; my brother was seen standing up and staggering with blood pouring from his many wounds.

All those witnesses told a true account of what happened that night – yes, some details differed, as they will invariably when told from different perspectives, but all their stories arrived at the same conclusion. Jade Braithwaite had been in Shillibeers with a few friends that night when a dispute had broken out between their group and another set of boys. My brother wasn't involved in this dispute at all, nor in any fighting that resulted as a consequence of it. Braithwaite and his friends were chased away and that should have been the end of it – what had been a stupid argument that led to a bar brawl (although quite a vicious one) and resulted in one of Braithwaite's friends being injured, should have died down after Braithwaite's group had left. Had it done so, my brother would still be here today. Instead, it was obvious that Braithwaite couldn't deal with being 'disrespected', couldn't take the fact that he'd lost face, and so he'd phoned a close friend, Michael Alleyne, who lived in the same street as Shillibeers, and asked him to come down and 'back him up'. Alleyne was with another friend, Juress Kika, and they quickly made their way down to the bar, eventually meeting up with Braithwaite, who had circled back to find them. Unfortunately, they walked up the road at the same time that my brother and a group of friends had decided to try and get a cab home. The defendants began chasing the boys and, according to witnesses, were shouting out to people along the way that someone was 'going to die that night' and that someone was 'getting shanked' – a street term for being knifed.

To this day, I still don't know why my brother stopped running. I wish to God he hadn't. Whatever his reasons – and I still believe it was simply to get out of the way of the oncoming trouble – he slowed down and crossed the road away from his friends. Deciding he was the easier target, the three men followed him and approached him. A witness testified that the only thing my brother said was, 'Why are you coming to me? I haven't done anything wrong,' before he was booted in the stomach, attacked with fists and stabbed eleven times.

Ben then found the strength to stand back up after their attack and walk across the road, looking down at his wounds and shaking his head sadly. The one time I had to leave the court was when one witness said that Ben slowly walked up to him and said, 'I've been stabbed, I've been stabbed,' repeatedly. I couldn't comprehend what my brother must have been feeling then.

This was the nearest to the truth we were ever going to

get as to what had happened that night and it was basically what we had been told all along. There were no surprises, no twists in the tale, no blame put on my brother in any of the witness accounts. Virtually all of the witnesses adhered to this story, and it was corroborated with CCTV footage of the road and forensics, blood splattering, etc. However, it didn't stop the defence team from giving our witnesses a hard time. The way they were treated was despicable.

Many of these witnesses were young kids – sixteen- or seventeen-year-olds who'd been brave enough to stand up for Ben, yet they faced being ripped to shreds in court. The lawyers made them feel bad for being out at a bar when they were underage, brought up silly misdemeanours, such as previous fights or minor drug possessions, to try and discredit them, and basically twisted their words until they almost gave up. Some of them cried, some of them, inevitably, got angry. It was really unfair, seeing these trained, intelligent lawyers from privileged backgrounds pit their wits against young kids who had no experience of the legal process, but I'm proud to say that all of them held their own.

The worst thing was that because they were underage and were petrified of the defendants, and rightly so, seeing as we had all heard how they were going to 'sort out any snitches', the court had issued special measures so that many of the witnesses were given a screen to give evidence behind and had been promised anonymity. The police had assured them that only their first names would be read out in court and this was the only way they could get many of them to agree to stand up. Yes, they all wanted to help Ben, but at what cost to them or their own family's safety? It seemed a small thing to ask for privacy.

As it turned out, it didn't happen – the lawyers gave out witnesses' full names, to the point where the kids were crying in fear and threatening not to give evidence at all. They apologized but I found it inexcusable that these educated, erudite individuals, who are paid a great deal of money not to make mistakes, could find it so difficult to remember this one condition. At times it seemed to me they knew they were rattling the witnesses, making them angry, making them want to go home and give up, and the more it happened the angrier I got. When one witness got so upset that they said on the stand, 'It's not you who has to go back home, it's not you who has to walk the streets,' one lawyer even had the audacity to reply, 'I assure you your safety will not be compromised.' As if he could guarantee that; as if he had any idea what it was like to live in these kids' worlds. Eventually, the judge gave a ruling to ensure the press didn't print any of the witnesses' full names but I felt the damage had already been done. At the very least, it could make the job of the police much harder when they tired to obtain witness testimonies in future cases.

It was also annoying when the defence kept trying to discredit the witnesses by saying they were all Ben's close friends and were simply covering for him. This wasn't true. Ben had a group of three or four best friends and unfortunately not one of them was there that night. Many of the witnesses I had never heard of before, had never even heard Ben mention. The truth was he wasn't close to any of them. They were simply doing the right thing and telling the truth.

Despite their treatment, nearly all the witnesses tried their best and there were even some surprise appearances – individuals who I never in a million years dreamed would be on our side. Early on in the case, a young girl, who we were told was Alleyne's cousin, had given a brief statement to the police confirming that Alleyne had fled to her house immediately after the murder, as he obviously wanted to get out of the area to avoid being caught. He had brought his friend Kika with him and she claimed they had stayed for a couple of days, not saying or doing much, nor even explaining why they were there.

Her account didn't really help the case much. However, when Alleyne found out that she'd spoken to the police, he got extremely angry and sent her nasty letters from prison that she took offence to and showed to the police. She then decided to tell the full story and admitted that she had left out many details in her previous statement. She now said that Alleyne and Kika had both admitted being there that night but, more importantly, that they had both admitted to stabbing Ben. They even tried to count the number of times they'd stabbed him between them and had reached a total of eleven. She also said that she heard Alleyne on the telephone discussing getting rid of a weapon. We were worried that she was simply saying all this just because Alleyne had written such spiteful things to her but, thankfully, she had admitted the truth to her mum soon after the murder, who had given an almost identical account to the police.

Once Alleyne heard what she'd said, he became even more vicious, threatening her safety and calling her every name under the sun. In a letter that was read out in court he wrote:

To Slag aka snitch, you are a let down to the family. You are not my cousin, believe that. How are you gonna give my letters to the Boyden [police] and be snitching on me? You are not real at all. When will I see you? Your mum's still on road, so be careful how you move. You don't know how I move on road. I'm a boss. I don't know who the fuck you are, you don't try to keep me out of jail. You all best hope I don't bust case because people will be in trouble and you will never snitch on anyone again, I promise you that. Say no more, I am ghost. I ain't got time to rite to snitches, family that's not real. I got your statements, everyone will see you are a snitch. You see, snitches get touched. All the family know you are a snitch so if I get found guilty it's down to you.

It was funny how he kept using the word 'snitch', which on the street means 'grass' and never liar – something that our lawyer used to try and prove his guilt.

Instead of scaring her, Alleyne's letters made his cousin even more determined to give evidence against him and she bravely took the stand, despite not getting any favours or rewards for it and despite having his family up in the public gallery looking on. She was an essential witness for us and even though it must have been extremely hard, she stood up and did what was right, unlike the rest of Alleyne's family.

His dad and his sister had given early accounts to the police that were quite damning for Alleyne – his dad had admitted that Alleyne had gone out just before the estimated time of the murder and arrived home shortly after and his sister had handed over a pair of his jeans and said that he'd asked her to 'get rid of them'. These jeans were later found to have Ben's blood all over them. They had signed statements to this effect, yet when they were called to the stand they completely changed their stories. They even suggested that the police had added bits to their statements after they had signed them. Although it was obvious Alleyne had pressured them to do this, and it was clear they didn't want to see their son and brother go away for many years, I couldn't believe that a decent human being would try to cover up a murder, especially after looking at the devastated faces of my family across the court.

In fact, it's sad to say that most members of the defendants' families acted disgracefully and made what was already a horrific ordeal for us a hundred times harder. I had never expected any kind of help from them, nor did

I honestly expect them to hand over their sons willingly for appropriate punishment, although I knew what my mother would have done and what many brave mothers *have* done in cases such as these.

I did, however, expect some sort of remorse or shame or embarrassment. No matter what their sons or relatives had told them about their involvement, once you'd heard most of the early evidence, any sane person couldn't help but know the truth. When they knew the circumstances of my brother's murder, when they knew how violently and brutally he had been attacked, when they could see how much we were suffering, I really expected them finally to understand the atrocity of what their offspring had done.

What I didn't expect was the intimidation, the violence and the pure nastiness that certain members of their families put us through. Bad enough to get on the stand and change your story for your relation – that, at a very big push, I could understand. But to physically attack my friends and family, to spit on them and call them 'scum' and other disgusting names, to sing 'who let the dogs out' as we walked by, to have the audacity to tell my dad to 'walk away and have respect' – this I could never, ever understand. Their behaviour was despicable. My family had done nothing to them – it was their relations who had taken something so precious away from us – but rather than put their heads down and try to get through this with even an ounce of the dignity my family had shown, they instead decided to show their true nature.

The saddest thing was that you could see where these boys had got it from – they'd never had a chance of growing up to be decent members of society considering they'd been brought up with influences such as this. We tried not to let it get to us, we tried to laugh it off, but our anger was building and every time we complained or reported them, we were told that the CCTV showed nothing and that they had been warned and it wouldn't happen again. Yet every day they were back in the public gallery, back outside the court, following and threatening us. It came to a head the day that one of them apparently said about my brother, 'So what? He's dead anyway.' This was said to one of Ben's best friends and when he lost his temper in fury and began swearing and shouting back, a male relation of theirs walked over and grabbed him by the throat and threw him against the wall. Once again we complained but this intimidating individual was back again the next day.

It is these indignities, these injustices, that made the process that much harder for us. We were going through enough – having to listen to every detail of Ben's wounds, having to hear that one stab was delivered so forcefully that it split his rib bone was bad enough, but when we came out at lunch to get away from it all and were faced with this awful bullying and aggression, it was too much.

It was fine if the authorities kept missing it on CCTV (though you'd have thought our word and complaints time and time again should have been good enough), it was fine if they couldn't monitor outside the court, but there were many things that they could have changed or controlled to improve the situation. There was no segregation in the public gallery, which meant members of my family had to be seated with theirs, and it was then that the tension and aggression began to build. This could have been avoided simply by having a divider or more security, but no one in authority seemed to listen to us.

This was a feeling we had almost the whole way through the trial process. If it hadn't been for our wonderful lawyers and police team, we would have had no idea what was going on. It was as if we were invisible as Ben's family, as if we didn't matter, as if no one wanted to acknowledge us or what we had been through. We had to sit at the back of the court where it was hard to see and hear everything, we were told not to look at the jury, not to look at the defendants – basically not to make our presence felt.

My sister Jade was the volatile one and if she was ever caught trying to catch a glimpse of the faces of the men who'd killed her brother she was told off and warned she wouldn't be allowed back in court, yet their families could physically and verbally attack us with no consequences whatsoever. It seemed wrong – it was all about giving a fair trial to the defendants, but when would anyone recognize the injustice that had been done to us?

It dragged on for seven long weeks and only certain things now stick out in my mind. Hearing them talk about Ben's wounds and measuring many of them at over sixteen centimetres long broke my heart; listening to the way his blood splattered on the road and on to the boys, and discovering that Alleyne had had seventy-two spots of Ben's blood on his jeans broke it further; but listening to two of the defendants give their accounts of what happened that night destroyed me completely.

Jade Braithwaite was the first defendant to take the stand, which seemed appropriate. In the early days, he had first answered any questions with a 'no comment', then later concocted a story saying that he knew nothing about the murder, and that after he and his friends had been chased away from the bar he'd gone straight to the hospital to get his friend checked out and had been nowhere near the scene of the crime. But eventually, after being confronted with evidence and witness reports that placed him there, he had come up with his final story. He said that he'd been standing in a car park trying to get into his friend's house when he saw a group of boys being chased up the road. He then hid behind a wall where he witnessed two boys, one of whom he knew as 'Tigger', grab Ben and stab him before running off. He claimed that, despite having changed his story numerous times, this was the truth. He named Alleyne as the stabber and put all the blame on him, swearing that he had taken no part in the brutal events.

In the covert tapes, Braithwaite spoke in street slang, swore and cussed over and over again and sounded like somebody who knew all about the criminal world. When he took the stand, he was primly dressed in shirts and sweater vests, spoke as if he'd taken elocution lessons and acted as if he was a poor innocent boy who didn't deserve to be there. He played on the fact that he had gone to college and had coached football in the past. His lawyer also felt it was important to mention that he hadn't had a relationship with his father for many years, as if this was a good enough excuse for murder.

He tried to say that he wasn't close to Alleyne and that he hardly knew Kika, even though it turned out he had grown up with Alleyne and that his younger brother was still his best mate. From the comfortable way they all spoke to each other in the van you could tell they were no strangers – this was a close group of friends.

Despite saying that his last version was the final one and the truth, Braithwaite changed his story once more when he took the stand. This time he claimed that as he'd been standing in the car park outside his friend's house, he'd seen my brother standing across the road with a few other people. He'd gone over to my brother and said, 'Don't worry, I'm not looking for trouble,' and had repeated this when my brother didn't answer him. He then claimed that Ben had stepped forward and swung a punch at him, and that he'd had to push him to the floor, where my brother had pulled him down and continued grappling with him. He then said that Alleyne and Kika ran up from nowhere and automatically began stabbing Ben without a word from him. He just stood back and watched and was horrified. He had never wanted that, he claimed.

This was the first time I felt complete hatred for this person. Despite never having mentioned my brother attacking him before, despite it being clear that he was blatantly lying now, and after everything he had done to my brother, he now had to try and defile his name and his reputation, to claim that Ben had attacked *him* when Ben wasn't here to answer or defend himself against these ridiculous lies. Anyone who knew Ben would know this wasn't true, but I couldn't bear people in the court or in the press even considering it. My brother would never have done that. He was five-foot-nine and Braithwaite was six-foot-six – he wouldn't have even been able to reach him.

Despite knowing the truth, I began to get scared. Braithwaite was good – he seemed too composed and the whole way through his testimony he kept his cool and spoke intelligently, giving such a good performance that I was petrified the jury would believe him. At no time did he show any remorse or accept any blame, and even when his own lawyer asked if he felt at all responsible for Ben's death, he shrugged and said, 'No, not at all.' Although he never convinced me with his absurd stories, I worried that there was a possibility he could get away with what he'd done, and this sickened me.

This worry abated slightly when Alleyne took the stand. Whereas Braithwaite was very formal and looked and spoke like a decent boy, Alleyne was the complete opposite. He made no effort with his clothes, simply wearing jeans and a crumpled T-shirt, nor did he make any effort when addressing the jury, most of the time issuing nothing but a grunt and not even trying to look as if he cared. It was obvious he didn't. He knew what he'd done and he must have known he would be going away for it, but he didn't even try to help himself. From what he had said in the covert tapes, 'At the end of the day, I'm still going home', you could tell a jail term meant nothing to him, no matter how lengthy. The one good thing he did do was dispense with the lie that Braithwaite had had no part in what had happened. He was obviously angry at having all the blame directed at him and 'snitched' on Braithwaite just as much. He fully admitted being present at the scene but said it was only because Braithwaite had called him and asked him to come and help, and that it was Braithwaite who'd reached Ben first and knocked him to the ground, and even though he'd joined in and punched Ben, at no time did he have a knife or see one. Again, he showed not one ounce of remorse or sorrow – not that this would have made us feel any better but I just couldn't understand the behaviour and attitudes of these boys – it was clear they had no compassion whatsoever.

Alleyne's wasn't the biggest admission of guilt but at least it placed him there and put Braithwaite back in the frame. Even though they were all blaming each other, even though none of them admitted to doing the actual stabbing, surely the jury would have to find them guilty of the murder, for there had been no one else there and my brother had died – whether it was one or all three of them that had stabbed him, they were all jointly responsible.

Kika didn't even bother to give evidence, something that the judge warned could go against him. He simply sat in the dock sneering and let his lawyers do all the work for him. This proved his guilt even more for me – surely if you were innocent the first thing you would want to do is protest this? However, I was also worried about the case against him, as Braithwaite had seemed to protect him all the way through, saying he didn't even know it was Kika there at the time and that he'd never seen him with a knife, and Alleyne also hadn't elaborated on his part in everything. There wasn't a great deal of forensics on Kika either, although he was the one who'd bragged most in the covert tapes, so I hoped this was enough.

And then it was all over. There was nothing more to be heard. The lawyers all made their closing speeches and hearing every one was like a roller-coaster ride. Our lawyer made you believe that all three were jointly guilty beyond a doubt, but then every time a defence lawyer got up and delivered an opposing shot, I felt my heart sink – they were just as convincing.

Finally, the judge summed the case up in his own words and ordered the jury to go out and find a rightful verdict. The most frightening point was when he stressed that if there was 'any reasonable doubt in their minds', any doubt at all that these boys were guilty, then the verdict must reflect that. I walked out of the court shaking with fear. At that point, I honestly didn't know what our chances were.

Chapter 16

I walk in and find you asleep.

This isn't unusual – you're always getting into trouble for being asleep when you should be doing much more important things. There's a running joke we have that you could fall asleep any time, any place. It's hard to wake you to tell you off, though, as you make sleeping look like an art – spread diagonally across any space, arms and legs everywhere, usually with one pet or another draped across you and the most beautiful, peaceful smile on your face. I wouldn't want to wake you then.

But this is very different.

I walk in to find you asleep but you're not in your own bed. And instead of being sprawled out, reaching for as much space as your skinny body can cover, you are lying completely stiff and still. And instead of having one of your beloved pets to keep you company, there are wires and machines and bandages. And instead of looking beautiful and peaceful, you look like you're having a terrible nightmare. I really want to wake you up now.

And so I do.

I whisper your name and kiss you gently, finding my way through the wires and the wounds. You don't respond and I'm scared for a second. I worry that something has gone wrong but then you slowly open your eyes and the look of pain is replaced by that beautiful, beautiful smile.

We all crowd round you and we cry and we sob and we thank God that you're OK. We thank God that you were one of the lucky ones, that you have survived this horrific attack.

We soak up every bit of you, so conscious that we almost lost you forever, that your story almost had a different, untimely ending.

Your face and body are ghost white and the only bit of colour we can see are your freckles, but beneath the white, beneath the bandages, beneath the smell and terror of this awful, awful place, we start to find you again.

We rotate around you, touching every part of you, kissing every bit of you, covering every inch of you with our tears. You laugh weakly and insist you are fine, say that it only hurts a little bit, that it could have been a lot worse.

You're trying to be brave for us but I can see the fear in your eyes, hear the tremor in your voice, feel the shock coming off your little body in waves. You are petrified, you were petrified; you thought you were going to die back there but you are here now, where you belong, with the people that love you, and we will never let anybody hurt you again.

Our hysterical tears turn into hysterical laughter as the relief that you are really OK sets in. You start to tell us what happened, to try and make sense of what they did to you and why, but we tell you not to worry – we'll deal with that later.

It will take a long time to get over this but we'll get there in the end. We'll take you home and look after you and shower you with love and goodness until all the evil has been chased away. Eventually the fear and the pain and the shock will go and you'll chalk it up as experience. It will make you stronger and wiser and, although you will never forget what happened, although the horrific scars will always be there as a reminder, you will just be grateful that you survived, that you were able to go on and live the life you were meant to.

We take you home and put you in your own bed, wrap you in your duvet safe and warm and stay with you until you finally fall asleep.

I go to bed and thank God again for saving you, for letting me keep my little brother, and I promise that I will never take Him for granted again. I will never take life for granted again, for it is precious, and I have learned a terrible but valuable lesson. I know that I'll have nightmares for the rest of my life but I finally fall asleep safe in the knowledge that you are only a floor above me, that you'll still be here in the morning. That you'll be here for many more years yet.

But then I wake up.

The verdict came in after an agonizing two-day wait, spent sitting outside a café across the road from the court sipping coffee after coffee as it was the only thing we could keep down. We were joined by around fifty family members and friends, all pacing up and down, many chain-smoking, as we waited for the most important decision of our lives.

It was early morning on Thursday 11 June and we'd only been at court an hour. We had just sat down and ordered our coffees when my mum got the phone call to say we had to get back to court immediately as the jury was in.

Funnily enough, my dad had guessed this would be the day, as many of the jury members were dressed smartly in suits and it had given us hope. We all rushed back to court, hugging and kissing family members for luck on the way.

As soon as we'd got the call, I burst into tears and couldn't control myself. Our chief detective, DCI John McDonald, told me not to worry and joked that we hadn't even heard the answer yet but I couldn't stop crying. This was it – the end of the road, the culmination of the most horrific year anyone could ever experience.

But at the end of the day, what did it all matter? Who cared what the answer was? Yes, if it was not guilty for any of them we would all be further devastated, all be right back to square one with no hope, no comfort and no one left to help us. But even if it was a guilty verdict, what did we really gain? Some would say justice but there was nothing anybody could give us that was worth what Ben had been and so it all suddenly seemed futile. All the hard work, all the worry, the sadness and the pain and the loss, for what?

Despite this, I couldn't bear to hear the words 'Not

Guilty'; couldn't bear any of them to go running back into the arms of their families, the families who had terrorized us for weeks on end; couldn't bear them to walk back on to the streets and hurt someone else's child.

We walked into that court as if we were walking towards our deaths. The judge entered solemnly and sat down and the jury members slowly filed in. The entire courtroom was packed, the public gallery was full, with many more people waiting outside the court, yet you could have heard a pin drop. The silence was excruciating. Although it was only minutes we waited, it felt like forever.

The court clerk stood up and asked the foreman of the jury to rise. A man dressed in his best suit, a man I had sneakily watched for almost two months (as I had every other jury member, searching them all for any signs or clues), stood up and even he looked scared. Was he scared of the reaction his answers would provoke from the defendants or from us, Ben's family?

First the clerk asked if the jury had reached a unanimous decision with regard to the three defendants, to which the foreman replied, 'Yes'.

She then asked, 'Do you find the defendant, Jade Braithwaite, guilty or not guilty of murder?' In the one second it took for him to answer, I nearly passed out in fear. Although all three were guilty of Ben's murder, for some reason I blamed Jade Braithwaite the most. It was he who'd been involved in the original dispute, he who'd called the other two out, he who'd sat there and lied and tarnished my brother's name, and he who I thought had the best chance of getting off.

'Guilty' came the reply. There were cries of 'Yes!' and cheers from the public gallery as the answer was announced. There were also cries of despair from his family. He, at least, had the grace to put his head down, though this was probably more from shock than remorse, as I think he also really believed he had a good chance of getting off. Once Braithwaite was found guilty, I was confident the other two would be as well, and the jury didn't disappoint. Alleyne and Kika were also declared guilty and the cheers and applause increased. They didn't react in any way, not even as the judge ordered them to be taken down to return for sentencing the next day.

It somehow seemed like an anticlimax. It was nothing like I had expected or had seen in films and was, in fact, finished in minutes. All that waiting for a ten-minute finale. I couldn't believe it was all over.

We walked out happy but in a daze and were surrounded by family and friends and the media, all waiting to hear our response to the verdict. Of course we were ecstatic, of course we were so grateful to the jury and to the police and our lawyers, Mr Hilliard QC and Mr Penny, for getting Ben some sort of justice, but it was still a bittersweet victory; it still felt empty. We also had to wait another day for the sentencing and so we couldn't really answer how we felt. Yes, they'd all been found guilty and would all be sentenced

to life imprisonment, but what if they each received a rec-
ommended minimum years? That wouldn't be any kind of
justice for us and so everything really depended on the sentence the judge passed the next day.

We were warned that the minimum tariff for murder
with a knife is fifteen years and told that it was unlikely
they would get more than eighteen years. This was higher
than the minimum of twelve years that had been passed in
previous cases, and though I wasn't sure if it was because
of a difference in the age of the defendants or simply
because they had started to get tougher on knife crime, I
was still horrified. I was hoping for at least twenty-five
years or more, which sounded much more proportionate
to the crime (although it still wouldn't be enough for me);
fifteen to eighteen years sounded like nothing. Ben had
only been with us for sixteen years; it was hardly more
than he had lived. If that time flew past for them like it had
for us since Ben died, they would soon be out, back in
society, able to carry on with their lives when my brother
never could – it didn't seem fair. The funniest thing was
that we were told if they'd attempted to rob my brother
before they murdered him they would have got a higher
sentence, but seeing as it was 'only murder' there were
certain guidelines that had to be adhered to. It was laugh-
able.

We returned the next day and before the judge made
his decision, the defence teams again tried to wrangle
their clients out of hefty sentences. It didn't matter that a

jury had found them guilty, they wanted them to serve the least time possible and tried to pull on heartstrings by blaming poor home lives, stating that *they* were in the 'wrong place at the wrong time', and even insisting that they were only young and should be allowed to make something of their lives when they got out. It was appalling to listen to and I walked out shaking with anger. Thankfully, the judge didn't seem to listen to any of their nonsense and, after taking a short break to deliberate, he came back and gave a very powerful closing speech. Finally, somebody was saying all the things we'd wanted to say for so very long.

He branded the defendants cowards and summed them up by saying, 'Your blind and heartless anger that night defies belief. Ben Kinsella had in front of him a lifetime of promise and you have taken all that away in a brutal, cowardly and unjustifiable attack. It reflects yet again the futility of carrying and using knives. Not a hint of remorse has been shown by any of you.' He added, 'His family will never get over it and he will never be forgotten.'

He spoke about Ben and what a wonderful boy he had seemed and, finally, the world got to learn about the actual victim of this horrific attack. My mum had been brave enough to stand up in court and read out an impact statement she'd written in which she described the pain of losing her only son. Her voice shook as she said, 'We as his family have been left devastated and in total despair. Our whole world has been totally turned upside-down. Ben went for a good night out and never came home again. Ben loved life, he loved living and he had so much to live for. He knew where he was going and where he wanted to be. Ben loved nothing more than to make people laugh; he was a fun-loving, happy-go-lucky boy with a heart of gold and would do anything for anyone.'

Even the jury cried as she read, 'The people who murdered him knew nothing about our Ben, not a hair on his head, a bone in his body, not anything about our wonderful son. They had never met him before or spoken to him – they just cruelly took his life away with knives for no apparent reason. We had brought Ben up to always walk away from trouble. This sadly cost him his life. He walked away to get safely home and they took advantage of that – he was one boy on his own.'

Finally as a family we got to express how we felt, the pain we had gone through. There were no more formalities or rules to hide behind – we were explaining exactly what these three brutal animals had done to our family.

She finished with, 'Our nights are filled with nightmares of our son's last moments and what he went through. We, as a family, will never get over the loss of our Ben. We are just trying to get through it. Our family faces a lifetime of feeling this way. All we can hope and pray for is that justice will prevail.'

After listening to her passionate statement and summing up all the relevant issues, the judge ordered the three defendants to serve a minimum of nineteen years before they were eligible for parole. He would have liked to have given them twenty but took a year off on account of their ages.

As they were led from the dock for the final time, the public gallery broke into applause and cheering, which the defendants didn't take kindly to. They turned around and sneered and even made gun gestures with their hands, while their families shouted abuse and spat at whoever they could reach. For once their behaviour wasn't enough to upset us and we actually laughed at them and the piti-ful people they were. I didn't ever want to have to see any of their faces again, especially the defendants. Although I was sure they would haunt me until my dying day, I was determined to try and get them out of my mind. In fact, it was one of the reasons I decided against having their mugshots included in this book. I didn't want to immor-talize them or give them any more notoriety than they'd already had, especially not in something that was a tribute to my brother. I felt their likenesses would taint Ben's story. Anyone who needs to see them can find numerous photos in the media and online. I myself never again want to gaze into their cold eyes and see the utter contempt they hold for human life.

My family walked out of the court holding hands to be met by frenzied applause from the public. Again the media wanted to know how we felt and we tried to process and put into words all that had happened. Yes, nineteen years was better than eight or ten, but could we still really call it justice? I was grateful to the judge, as it was clear he'd wanted to punish them more harshly, but these were rigid laws he had to stick to. Apparently while the tariff for murder with a knife started at fifteen years, if you used a gun it started at thirty and this angered us – was there really that much difference between these two deadly weapons?

My fight against knife crime in the past year had focused on trying to find out why it was happening and looking for solutions to the problem. I still very much wanted to continue that work and I still wanted to prevent kids picking up knives and using them on other kids, and I wanted to take all I'd learned and put it into practice. However, after the trial I also found another cause.

Having gone through the horrific ordeal of the criminal justice process, there were many things I felt needed to change. Again, it was too late for my family, but I wanted to make things better for other families who may have to go through court processes in the future. My family and I also wanted to highlight the difference between gun and knife sentencing and try to get some changes implemented by the government. Although nineteen years was actually quite a long sentence in the current climate of lenient sentencing policies, the whole country was on our side in the belief that it wasn't enough.

First though, we had to have a rest and celebrate the small victory we'd won. My family and friends, our wonderful police team and the jury all gathered in a pub near the court and, even though it was early afternoon, we all raised our glasses to Ben and hoped he was happy with the verdict. We couldn't stop thanking the jury, although they wouldn't accept our gratitude and simply said they were doing the job they'd been given.

The same went for the police, who were just happy that all their hard work had been rewarded with a conviction. As we all said our goodbyes, it seemed strange that these faces we'd got so used to over the past year, and in particular the past couple of months, wouldn't be around any more. They had almost become part of our lives and it would seem strange to be left on our own now, even though it was probably what we most needed as a family.

The next few days were a whirlwind of interviews with newspapers and the TV stations. My mum and dad had been quiet up until now, concentrating on grieving and getting justice for their son, but now it was all over they wanted to tell the world how they really felt. They were petrified, having never been in front of a camera before, and my mum couldn't stop shaking, but once they started talking, the words that came out were astounding.

If I had thought I'd interviewed well over the past year, it was nothing to what my mum and dad did. They spoke as parents, from the heart, and everybody sat up and listened. They said they didn't believe the punishment was enough and highlighted the difference between the tariffs, begging the government to address it and give us some reasons why. They appealed to every mum and dad out there, every parent who was living in fear for their children's safety. They did several interviews over the course of a few hours and by the time they got in the car to go home, Secretary of State for Justice Jack Straw had announced an emergency press conference and stated that he was going to conduct a review of sentencing. All that work I'd done in a year and my parents had managed to make the most enormous difference in a matter of hours! I was unbelievably proud of them and knew that, wherever Ben was, he would be too.

And finally, it all seemed to be over. There was nothing left for us to do. The trial was over, the case was closed, the government had heard our pleas and we were waiting for results. There was still a great deal of work to be done, we still had Ben's legacy to pass on and still wanted to make sure our streets and our kids were safe, but at this particular point in time, we had done all we could.

It seemed strange not to be busy, not to be fighting for something or working towards something. And this was when the grief hit us the hardest. Now it was quiet, now we were standing still, we could see how empty our lives were without Ben's presence. It hurt more than it ever had, especially as we were only days away from the first anniversary of his death.

Whatever we'd gone through in the past year, no matter how hard things had seemed, nothing was going to be tougher to get through than the coming week. After that, no longer could we say, 'This time last year he was still here, this time last year he was doing this . . .' It was time to finally wake up from this nightmare and realize that Ben really wasn't coming home. There could be no magical happy ending for us, no different outcome, he really was gone.

Chapter 17

Once again I awaken.

It's very different. I stand up and notice the beaming golden light that pierces my enriched eyes. No source of the light is clear. Just emitting light from beyond the horizon. I look down and press my wounds. They're still there, yet I feel no pain.

The soft, moist grass is a rich purple colour. Every blade cut at the same perfect angle. Yet every blade seems unique. It feels and sounds like I'm buried underwater like the poorly battle-ship, yet I'm clearly not. I'm neither breathing nor blinking. I just stand there and orientate myself. The buzzing and tweet-ing of a summer's day rounds off the atmosphere. It's pleasant. I know it's not real, yet, it is.

I look forward and find a typical old brown wooden house. It has a porch with an old rocking chair. The chair is meant for me. So is the house. But it soon becomes clear as I walk patiently towards it that I'm not getting any closer. My walk turns into a jog, which grows into a sprint.

My wounds begin to pulse and burn. Shrieking pain bulges from the cuts. I collapse in a heap. When I get to my feet I find myself, unexpectedly, outside the door. I feel no need to sit on the chair but feel the strangest urge to go inside.

Music now drowns the buzzing and the tweeting. I pull the door towards me to find myself in a situation I would never have imagined.

I'm in a full-blown rave! The floor is shaking. No sight in existence compares to the one I'm witnessing! There are numbers of people too high to count – a rainbow-coloured ocean of waving hands. They're all dancing. Dancing to the music. The never-ending beat. There are no speakers in sight. Just a forever flowing beat, it's impossible to get bored of. A short distance away lie vast tables that stretch like the desert. They are filled with luxurious, hearty food. Heavenly food. Now I know, I've reached my heaven.

On one of the huge tables, just on the very edge, I see something that made my tears climb to the edge of my already glistening eyes. My family and friends. Not the living ones, but loved ones I had lost. One by one their distant heads bob up like ripe red apples in a barrel of water. They wave. They shout. Beckoning. I bundle down the stairs as if I were a small child in a toy shop, wildest dreams becoming reality. I force my way through the crowd with sheer excitement and curiosity, then take a seat. The grand chair is soft and comforting. The smell of new leather wafts up my flaring nostrils.

'Ben, my boy.' As he spoke it felt like someone had turned the music down just so we could share this moment.

Why Ben?

'How you doing, son? Words can't describe how you must be feeling now but let me reassure you everything happens for a reason. All will be explained, son, just give it some time.' This warm, gruff voice belongs to the cheery face of my granddad Michael. The voice that soothed everybody's troubles. A voice you could trust and understand – that knew everything. I try to talk, but I seem unable.

'Don't worry, Ben, like I said, it takes time.' He acknowledges the fact that I can't speak. 'Your body hasn't fully shut down. In a short while you'll be able to do pretty much whatever you did when you were alive plus much, much more.' I nod to show I've understood. Much, much more, I think to myself? In the next few minutes what more could happen to my body?

White fire roars inside me. I'm so excited I can hardly think. Curiosity forces me to become extremely impatient as I can't help but question what these next few minutes will bring. As I look around the table I see other familiar faces. Aunties and uncles, childhood friends, even people from the pub who I only said hello to. I sit and listen to what people say to me. It's mainly things like 'we've missed everybody terribly', 'just my luck', and 'it had to happen some day'. And a few jokes are thrown in too.

It's just so pleasant. So wonderful. Although I am dead, I feel more alive then ever. They say time flies when you're having fun. Well here it's different, I'm having plenty of fun yet it seems like I've been sitting here for days on end. Time isn't in existence here, it doesn't need to be. I've long since _developed speech and we just sit and chat and eat and listen._

Finally I decide I want to explore this Milky Way, this heaven. I tell everyone I'll be right back – I just want to look around. As I stroll around the never-ending dance floor I see things that give me a wild mix of fascination and confusion. Things that would seem impossible. But this is heaven, right? Anything is possible here.

The ceiling is invisible to the naked eye, it stretches higher than the sky, space, higher than anything . . . floating platforms raised hundreds of feet into the soft air. I can just make out the young people having the time of their lives. Or deaths.

Death. It's not present here. It never will be. It's so alive. It feels and smells like I'm outside on a glorious summer's day in the middle of a beautiful countryside. Yet the reality is I'm stuck in the middle of the most vast and exciting rave I've ever witnessed. Pure electricity fills us all. It's more than I would expect even God to think up. It's fantastic. Wildly tamed. Nobody sleeps. You let the music and the people and the atmosphere and the feelings just sweep you away to a place you've longed to be. Everybody's in their very own heaven.

See, it's funny. I sort of imagined heaven would be a lot different. Through the years of listening to churchgoers babbling on about how heaven's a big fluffy cloud. Clustered with old people and angels donning golden harps. Then in the distance would be the giant, floating head of God with a huge white beard. I had the impression it would be exactly that. But, it's nothing of the sort. The people are all dressed in normal clothes. The clothes they died in.

Why Ben?

They are all just your average people and although God can't be seen, He can be felt. We know He is with us. He is all around. As He was when I was alive. He was also there when I died.

I have died. This is the first time I have properly thought about what had happened. Stood in the middle of thousands. I gaze blind into nothingness. Just thinking hard. Time seems to stop, everything stops. No one is here. Just me and my thoughts. Here they tell me my life had been taken. I will never be able to contact or communicate with anyone alive ever again.

And although this has happened to me, strangely, I don't feel the slightest bit angry. I just feel free. Free from anger, worries, anguish and pain. In retrospect, I had this burning desire to hate the animal who took me away from life. Yet, although I don't know why, I've forgiven the murderer.

So what will come next for me? God knows. I don't. But for now, I'll return to the table that my family humbly sit at. This is my home now, and I've never felt better. I'm not scared any more. There's no weight on my shoulders. No struggle. From now on I can do whatever I want whenever I want. I'll never say I'm glad He did it because, well, I'm simply not. But I much prefer it here than being stuck on a weird world. Let's just see what a future here brings. But at the moment, this is living. Not death.

By Ben Kinsella

Today it is the first anniversary of my brother's death. He has been gone for exactly a year and although it still feels like I saw him just yesterday, sometimes it seems as if we never had him at all. I count down the hours he had left on this earth and I send myself crazy. 'This time last year he was eating his last McDonald's . . .' 'This time last year he was doing his hair for the last time . . .'

I picture him opening the fridge for the last time, walking out our front door for the last time, hugging me goodbye for the last time, and it is these thoughts that break me. It isn't picturing him dead in the hospital, or lying cold in the morgue, or imagining his last terrifying moments – it's the little things. Picturing him doing the little things that made him happy, that made him Ben, not knowing that he wouldn't be here to do them tomorrow.

I can't believe that I haven't seen my baby brother for a year, that I will never see him in this life again. I haven't let myself really think about what that means and how much it's going to hurt but now that it's been a year, now that I can't say that this time last year he was still alive, I let the grief come.

Ben is really dead. He is never, ever coming home. He was murdered – painfully and brutally for no reason whatsoever. My parents have lost their son. My siblings and I have lost our cherished brother. Ben has lost his future.

I cry, really cry. This time I don't stop myself after a few minutes, don't block it out and put it to one side or put on a brave face. I cry for my lost brother, for my broken family and for all the pain and devastation those three cowardly men have caused. They will never fully understand the consequences of their actions that night, never understand what they denied this world when they took Ben. I am not being egotistical for I know in my heart that my brother was a special boy who would have gone on to be an amazing man. He would have made a mark in this world – but maybe this was the way it was always meant to be. Maybe this really was his destiny, his way of making a difference – a small comfort but not much. Why him?

We don't want to do anything on this horrible day, don't really even want to acknowledge it, but of course we have to. Our family priest holds a beautiful mass for Ben and once again the church is packed. There is not a dry eye after the service and everybody is given a 'Ben' candle to take home and light when they want to remember him.

In the early hours of the morning, around the time he was attacked, I make my way up to that haunting spot to light a candle for him. When I arrive, there are so many people standing there with their own candles and flowers, so many people who have come out even at this late hour just to pay tribute to my brother, that again I start to cry. The crowd falls silent, without a word from anybody, and we all say our own prayers and send our thoughts to Ben. The road is lit up with twinkling lights and for a second it looks so beautiful and seems so peaceful that it's hard to imagine the violence that was occurring here a year ago. I can't help but sit in the spot where he collapsed and will things to have gone differently. Though I know nothing can be changed, I still can't help but wish. This time last year Ben had five hours left to live, was being rushed to hospital in an ambulance while his heart struggled to stay alive.

I go home to my family and we stay up late and drink and dance, and cry and sing, and talk about Ben as much as we are able. We stay up until seven in the morning, and watch the clock tick down to Ben's last minute. It's almost as if we don't want to go to sleep because we know that when we wake up tomorrow it is the start of something new. It is the start of life without Ben. We haven't been living for the past year, we have simply been existing, but now it's time to try. None of us wants to 'move on' but Ben would want us to. It's not going to be easy but we know that we have to do it for him. We have got through the darkest days and survived the many occasions that we thought would be impossible and if we can do that then we can do anything. It has been the worst experience of our lives – Ben's murderers have ruined our lives forever – but I am so proud of my family for getting through it. I know that every one of us at one point has thought about giving up, has wanted to end the pain right then and go and be with Ben, but we didn't let them beat us, we are still here.

Why Ben?

It's not a case of just deciding to move on, though – it's not that easy as we don't know where we want to go to. Nothing in life excites us any more; we've lost all our dreams and hopes and ambitions. We don't know what to do with ourselves. Of course we'll all have to go back to work simply to survive, but none of us can even think about having an actual career. If you'd told me a year ago how much my life would change and that I'd be spending my time campaigning and fighting for justice rather than auditioning for acting jobs and partying with my friends, I would have laughed at the sheer ridiculousness of it. The one small good thing I can take away from this year is that I now know what matters in life. When I think of how I would cry at the stupidest things and get upset if I didn't get a particular job or had a silly argument with my boyfriend, I can hardly believe it. Those days when feeling a bit fat or not having much money felt like the end of the world are a lifetime ago. I now know what the end of the world really means so, if anything, the past year has brought me great clarity. Everything seems so shallow and pointless and while part of me wants to do nothing with my life, another part of me wants to make the most of every day I live, for my brother – to fill my life with all the experiences that he'll never get to have so that when I finally see him again, I'll have many stories to tell him and he'll be proud of me.

I have no idea what path my life will take now but

there is one thing I know for certain – no matter what I do, I will make sure that my brother is never forgotten and that his life and his death will count for something. It's the least I can do – for him and every other child we have lost in this awful way. I don't know how and I don't know if I will succeed – we've made some small but very important changes already but it's not enough. Kids are still being knifed every day and families and hearts are being broken, so I will do all I can to help.

I still don't know if my brother is OK. It's all any of us want to know. It's what keeps us lying awake at night in the dark, praying and begging for an answer. If we knew that he's OK and that he's happy, maybe we could feel some small comfort. I know that it would allow me some peace. But he hasn't sent me any signs – he hasn't popped by for a visit, in reality or a dream, and I don't ever hear his voice or smell his distinctive boy scent in the wind. I know I could go and see a medium and that maybe they could find him for me, but I don't want to be told a load of nonsense because they think that's what I want to hear. I know that he will come and find me when he's ready.

That's if he can. If there really is life after death and he's moved on to somewhere better. I know that's what we have to hold on to for our lost loved ones but, if I'm honest, I'm still not sure. What if the end really is the end and he is just in that cold ground, gone forever? I worry that this is the truth but then I have to believe that it is not – that there is a God and He wouldn't let such a wonderful person go to waste. If I am ever to get any kind of peace, I have to picture Ben somewhere in his heaven, in his never-ending rave as he described above.

Every time I read Ben's vision of heaven I can't help but smile through my tears. The fact that he was creating his idea of heaven just months before he died breaks my heart, but then it sounds so lovely, so perfect for Ben, that I have to smile and believe that it's true. I hope with every bit of my heart that he's up there among family and friends, feasting on his delicious food and dancing away to his beloved music.

If I could talk to Ben one last time, if I had the chance to see him just for a minute, I would tell him that he was the best little brother a girl could ever ask for. I would tell him that he made my life so much fun and that I will never again find anybody who will make me laugh like he did. I would tell him that I love him more than he could ever know and that I wished I had told him that more often.

That would be enough for me. If I could just tell him those important things I would be happy, so I have to hope that one day I'll get the chance, whether it's in this life or the next.

For now, I will just be grateful for the time I had with him and if you gave me the choice, if you told me that we could have been spared all this pain, that Ben could have been spared all that suffering just by never being here at all, I would still take it. I would go through every day of heartbreak again and again, just to have the privilege of being Ben's sister.

Acknowledgements

Firstly, a huge thank you to my wonderful editor Kerri Sharp, for having the faith in me and in Ben's story. All I wanted was to tell the world about my baby brother and you made that happen, so thank you.

Another big thank you to all the team at Simon & Schuster for their hard work and invaluable input into this book – I have felt very safe in your hands.

Thanks to Piers Blofield, Caroline de Wolfe and Rosemary Reed who helped set me on the right path and to Neil Ransome and Steadfast Television, who were with me every step of the way.

To all the inspirational people and organizations I have met in the past year, that have helped shape my journey and this book – thank you. I hope my writing did you justice.

A long overdue thank you to my wonderful boyfriend Ray, who has the patience of a saint – I love you.

And finally, to everybody up and down the country and across the world who has supported my family and helped campaign for justice – we thank you from the bottom of our hearts.

The Ben Kinsella Trust

After Ben was murdered on 29th June 2008, his family set up a charity for him named 'The Ben Kinsella Trust.' Since his death, the Trust has received many generous donations and plans to use its funds to pass on the legacy of Ben, to promote knife-crime awareness, to help support other anti-knife crime charities and projects, and to hopefully one day build a youth centre in Ben's name – as a tribute to him and to help protect, support and educate the kids on our streets.

If you would like any more information on the Trust, or would kindly like to give a donation please go to
www.benkinsella.org.uk

Or alternatively contact
Rob Graham
Graham Associates (International) Ltd
International Accountants
212 Piccadilly
London
W1J 9HG
robertgraham1@aol.com

(Please note that 100% of all donations will go towards the charity's work)

We thank you for your generosity and support.